"As American Christianity changes, and as we change along with it, we need guides to remind us who we are and who we're not. Sara has been one such guide for me. She's brutally honest and hilarious, and her heart is wide open to the radical possibility that belonging to Jesus is identity enough for Christians. I couldn't be more grateful for her."

Jon Guerra, singer-songwriter and producer

"I needed this book. I have no glowing words of endorsement, no pithy comments of promotion; I just have this: Sara and I, we overlapped like a Venn diagram in the themes of this book—the wrecking of our childish understanding of theology, the intentions gone wild, the incredulity of what it means to be a child and an orphan simultaneously. I needed this book, and I am grateful it is now in the world."

Lore Ferguson Wilbert, author of *A Curious Faith* and *Handle with Care*

"Billups reminds us that no matter who we are or where we come from, God can move us from a place on the margins to a community of faith. She calls us forward, with deep care for the people of God."

Foxy Davison, educator and activist

"This is the book you've been waiting for: the book that addresses those who love Jesus but find themselves disoriented by the ways he is wielded and weaponized in halls of power. This is a book for those who mourn the disconnect between the American church complex and the Bride of Christ. Half journalist, half mystic, Sara reminds us we are not alone and helps us move forward with the greatest gift: hope."

Erin Hicks Moon, writer and podcaster

"I wept as I read Sara Billups's *Orphaned Believers* because so much of her story is similar to my own. And though the similarities are daunting, the grace and wisdom she dispenses is exhilarating and so totally relieving. She proposes that there is a legitimate way forward for followers of Jesus. If you have been made weary by too many conspiracy theories and the outrage thereof, I invite you to feast on the grace and wisdom in *Orphaned Believers*. There is a balm for those of us connected, whether intimately or at a distance, with the American church. Sara Billups's voice is one that, if we are willing, will prophetically point us beyond the various problematic ideologies that have held us hostage to a life led by the Holy Spirit and toward the tender, merciful ways of Christ."

Andy Squyres, musician and writer

"'There's wilderness in all of us,' Sara writes. 'We're lost and found a little every day.' And in her honest-but-hopeful reflections, Sara helped me feel just a bit more 'found' than I did before—orphaned but also anchored in a much better story than the one the world's been selling me over the past decades. I needed this book more than I knew."

Chuck DeGroat, author, therapist, and professor of pastoral care and Christian spirituality at Western Theological Seminary

ORPHANED BELIEVERS

ORPHANED BELIEVERS

HOW A **GENERATION** OF **CHRISTIAN EXILES** CAN FIND **THE WAY HOME**

SARA BILLUPS

BakerBooks

a division of Baker Publishing Group
Grand Rapids, Michigan

© 2023 by Sara Billups

Published by Baker Books
a division of Baker Publishing Group
PO Box 6287, Grand Rapids, MI 49516-6287
www.bakerbooks.com

Printed in the United States of America

Library of Congress Cataloging-in-Publication Data
Names: Billups, Sara, 1978– author.
Title: Orphaned believers : how a generation of Christian exiles can find the way home / Sara Billups.
Description: Grand Rapids, MI : Baker Books, a division of Baker Publishing Group, 2023. | Includes bibliographical references.
Identifiers: LCCN 2022020839 | ISBN 9781540902436 (paperback) | ISBN 9781540903006 (casebound) | ISBN 9781493439584 (ebook)
Subjects: LCSH: Generation X—Religious life. | Christianity and culture.
Classification: LCC BV4529.2 .B55 2023 | DDC 261—dc23/eng/20220720
LC record available at https://lccn.loc.gov/2022020839

The author is represented by the literary agency of The Bindery Agency, www.TheBindery Agency.com.

Baker Publishing Group publications use paper produced from sustainable forestry practices and post-consumer waste whenever possible.

23   24   25   26   27   28   29   7   6   5   4   3   2   1

For Tom

CONTENTS

INTRODUCTION

I will not leave you as orphans; I will come to you.

John 14:18

Father, Son, and Holy Spirit. Coriander seeds and cilantro. The seed of a baby and a fleshy face. I thought my countercultural faith and my dad's faith were different, and I discovered that, all along, they were really the same.

But the Christianity he passed down to me wasn't enough to keep me steadfast.

In the '70s, Jesus People and young evangelical converts like Dad tried to start a revolution inspired by an eschatology predicated on the quick return of Jesus, but its fervor eventually fizzled. By the time I was a kid in the opulent '80s, my parents attended a cookie-cutter nondenominational suburban church and had traded ideals of a radical faith for a cul-de-sac.

Still, I stayed a Christian after being raised by a Jewish-turned-evangelical father so steeped in end-times prophecy that he told me I wouldn't grow up and start a family before the world ended.

I stayed a Christian after my college pastor, a former Jesus Movement hippie, taught me God would make any dream real if I asked.

11

Like the flesh of an orange turning purple from mulling wine, the blood of the Lamb would permeate any idea if I truly believed.

I stayed a Christian after we followed that pastor's theology and tried to start an intentional community in Seattle. And I stayed a Christian for the decade after, while watching many friends leave the church. In those years, I began to understand a left-behind feeling. I was treading in the same church waters while others were riding waves to an evolving or estranged faith. I did not feel set apart or hidden with Christ. It was a time of isolation and quiet, and I held a constant, sometimes physical unsettledness—the feeling of carrying a heavy bag over my shoulder when there was really just air.

Sometimes, in those years, I stayed a Christian by choice. Sometimes I stayed because I realized being a Christian wasn't contingent on my striving. It was, of course, about Jesus, and a small liberation came from removing myself from the center of the story. Sometimes I stayed a Christian by brute force. Because if I wasn't a Christian, where would my identity drift? Who would I become? Sometimes I stayed because the church held me up, or my husband held me up. Other times I stayed because I sensed God's quiet *hesed*, his loyal love, in the middle of the drought.

As it became increasingly hard to earn the social capital required to identify as a Christian in a city like mine in the early 2000s, I became two unequal halves. Each Sunday I attended a Presbyterian church. But I moved through the other days of the week with a threadbare prayer life and a fledgling belief in Jesus I rarely talked about to anyone besides my husband.

I was a middle-class, young, white woman living simply but well in Seattle's abundant, fresh air culture of farmers' markets, weekend hikes, and excellent coffee. In that season, reading the word *lukewarm* in the Bible caught my breath and tugged. I walked to the 11:00 a.m. service most Sundays and participated in a weekly small group. But I spent my week working in media, including marketing books for a small press and writing about food for an alt weekly.

There was no motivation to complicate my professional life by trying to explain to colleagues why I was still a Christian.

Mentioning Jesus at a Friday happy hour would have skidded the needle on the record and caused a few pint glasses to drop. Or at least that's how I imagined the scene. I got good at truncating my identity, and whenever God would tug through Scripture or prayer, I'd feel what might have been guilt or might have been conviction—but not enough of either to make me change. Looking back, I was self-soothing and in a state of young grief for a changing faith in a city that was skeptical of Christians for some good reasons. It took years for me to find even a little heat.

◆◆◆

Children of Boomer evangelicals like I am usually have a faith journey that looks a lot different from that of our parents' generation. While a 2014 Pew survey of Boomers found that 78 percent identify as Christians, and 69 percent were "absolutely certain" in their belief, just 57 percent of Millennials checked the Christian box, and only 52 percent were "absolutely certain."[1] Like me, many younger members of Gen X joined Millennials to form the generation after modernism and certainty. In the Seattle Metro Area where I live, 40 percent of residents in our thirties through fifties were "Nones,"[2] unaffiliated with any religion but "turning toward more individual forms of spiritualism."[3] Skeptical, postmodern, and increasingly postevangelical. And that was nearly a decade ago, before the presidency of Donald Trump.

People leave the church, be it the mega or home group variety, for any number of reasons. Some of us are exhausted from a life of required attendance and feel a sense of release when we leave an institution that has become mismatched with our adult identity. Some of us have experienced sexual, emotional, or spiritual abuse perpetrated by Christian leaders, and my God, it's next to impossible to keep attending a congregation where defenses are heightened instead of put to rest.

Introduction

A lot of us left the church because when we jumped, we fell. There was little spiritual formation taught on Sunday or at home. On our own in the world for the first time, we quickly lost our footing.

Still, some of us left because we were bored and because church didn't do anything for us. When the idealism of youth that many middle-class white kids are born with burns off, committing to Jesus when it is not personally aspirational has little appeal. As a general rule, affiliating with Christianity in a progressive American city is not good for personal brand.

During the Trump administration, the stack of reasons to leave the evangelical church grew much higher. For many, the word *evangelical* became synonymous with *white* and *Republican*. The Capitol insurrection, with its "Jesus 2020" banners and wooden cross propped up in a crowd of Christian nationalists, was grief-inducing for many Christians. Evangelicalism flavored by our parents' generation had become exclusionary to a lot of our peers. And with the rise of Christian nationalism and the calcification of cultural Christianity, the melting together of those ideologies became especially dangerous.

The undoing of American evangelicalism is a three-legged stool supported by politics, culture, and the market. *Orphaned Believers* explores how those stool legs began to wobble as a new generation of Christians grew up in the '80s and '90s. Our experience may also expand across different generations and ages to apply to many, regardless of age or generational affiliation.

◆◆◆

Many of us are questioning if it's worth staying in the church as we know it. The problem is, as hard as it may be, and with very few exceptions—captivity, a desert island—we can't fully experience Jesus without participating in some form of Christian community.

This book is for you, orphaned believer, weary from loss yet putting full hope in Jesus. It is also for you who have left church but remain compelled by the Christian story. Because the Spirit of God can work even, and especially, in our wandering.

14

Jesus says in John 14:18 that he will not leave us as orphans. Not orphaned from our parents' faith, our children's faith, or from the church. And I am convinced that we can bind ourselves together—and, when we need to, carry each other—toward the perfect love of Christ. In spite of how people we love may have been misguided. In spite of what social capital it costs.

Ultimately, I stayed a Christian because I came to believe, and experience, that Jesus's promise to not leave us as orphans holds true.

PART ONE
END TIMES

CHAPTER 1

Risky Business

Here is what you risk when choosing to give yourself over to the Christian story.

You will be called to believe Jesus was born of a virgin, turned water to wine, and was killed and then raised from the dead. Instead of such miraculous occurrences being mythology or symbol, you are convicted that these things really took place; if you happened to have been living two thousand years ago, you might have seen them with your own eyes.

Believing there is a living God—with a servant king Son and a Holy Spirit who dwells in your actual body—is a wild proposition.

As a Christian, you may be called to hope for impossibilities. To think thoughts that are both logical and intellectually aligned with science and your senses—while grappling with the possibility of holy visitations, physical healings, and the giving of spiritual gifts. You sign up for the whole story, even the mysterious or uncomfortable parts.

Believing in the Christian story also involves risk to your name. Christian conversion comes with claiming an identity that will almost certainly make you look out of touch to secular human-ists, atheists, the a-religious, the sacrilegious, and probably a few agnostics.

As Christians, we know what we sign up for, because Jesus told us plainly, "In this world you will have trouble" (John 16:33). Trouble beyond failing health, grief after losing a loved one, or financial hard-ship. Christian trouble reaches down into the middle of us, where our identity is being tugged at by the market, our current culture, and our own desire to win and be remembered.

To live as a modern American Christian, your belief in Jesus will also be pressed down by the past, by the historic church's bloody history and its bad actors who have skewed doctrine in every direc-tion. In the present day, the church's taint by nationalism and every-other-*ism* further complicates bearing Christian belief.

For some, however, this last bit is where things can start to get easy. Take the person identifying as a Christian who voted for Trump in 2016 or 2020. This person may or may not have internal con-flict about casting their vote for a president who co-opted Chris-tianity for the power of office. This person may believe the exchange was worth it and had little trouble overlooking President Trump's transgressions. People change. Nobody's perfect. Just look at King David.

The American church is not monolithic. There are some denomi-nations, and also particular churches within large denominations, that have been moving forward in an orthodox and beautiful expres-sion of faith in the midst of our culture wars.

But other churches have rested on the soft bed of cultural Chris-tianity and may not feel the need to wake up anytime soon. Because if your identity gives you access to power, comfort does not demand reformation. There are two ways to respond to the fear of change if you are culturally Christian but do not yet live a life marked by the transformation of Jesus: either you tighten your grip on the sheets, pull the covers to your chin, and try to sleep—or you get up and make the bed.

Today, there are a growing number of white Christians estranged from the dominant culture of the modern American church, specifically evangelicalism, in almost every way. I include myself among them. We believe whiteness has blinded the church to racism. That sexism has suppressed the gifts of women and propagated a culture of abuse. That sexual minorities have been banished instead of made welcome. That celebrity pastors have led churches with ambition, magnetism, and in many times deep moral failure.

Consumerism has stripped away the church's posture toward radical simplicity. Culture wars have severely damaged our credibility, as we have sought power through political posturing instead of spiritual formation.

I feel it in me—a pull toward exceptionalism. Of being glad to be one of the few on the right side of history. But the way of Jesus calls us to guard against believing we are "in" a remnant of true believers while others are "out." In reality, no matter what worldview we hold, the earnest Christian who holds the opposite opinion is just as much "in" Christ.

We all likely believe we're sitting on the right side of the vote and pew. Many of us have tender and personal stories of conviction that led us to our current beliefs. At times we might hear from God, think we hear from God—or assume if we did hear something, it would be God telling us to hold fast to our political and cultural posture. When we miss God, we may be seeing a reflection of us instead of submitting to a wholly other Creator.

The 2020 election took a neon highlighter and underlined not just what many of us stand against but what we stand for. It was also an invitation to remember that we are not called to judge another. In Matthew 7:2, Jesus says "in the same way you judge others, you will be judged, and with the measure you use, it will be measured to you." This command is always true and is especially resonant during a charged political era. In the case of the evangelical church, the Trump presidency put our opinions and convictions on hyperspeed. Yet in letting go of judgment, a joyful rebuilding of Christ's church and a great reconciliation of the saints is possible. Here, hope swaps out the suffocating scarcity of being on the right side of the culture wars.

After Jesus says we will have trouble in the world, there is a glowing lantern on a dark path: he tells us he has overcome the world. We will be estranged in our lives, but we are not to be defensive. Instead, we can choose to put our great hope in all being made right in the end.

That great hope can lead us to make changes now that move us a little closer to God's upside-down kingdom, where the first are last. Ordinary saints working quietly around the globe with contrite spirits will rise up to places of honor.

If I've learned anything over the past four decades, it is this: to live the Christian life well, to persevere, we have to accept the possibility that God is not just real but loving. Actively loving. Actively loving each of us. Which means change and restoration are possible.

What Is an Orphaned Believer?

God loves the sojourner. Deuteronomy 10:18 says, "He defends the cause of the fatherless and the widow, and loves the foreigner residing among you."

This book is for Christian sojourners. For orphaned believers.

The following chapters will attempt to answer the question, What happened to a generation of Christians who grew up in the church but are left weary and wandering?

Orphans don't find themselves orphaned by something they did. Who is the orphan-maker—the one who does the abandoning? Sometimes it's one or more persons in our life. Other times it's the church or community we grew up in. Often it's both.

When I talk about orphaned believers, I mean two things.

First, orphaned believers are cultural orphans. We're Christians in a middle space. We might be politically progressive, moderate, or conservative, but we have joined together in standing against the deep currents of Christian nationalism that surfaced during the Trump presidency. We are troubled by white nationalism's lasting implications for the American church. We're often alienated in our pursuit of Jesus in a moment when many people equate identifying as a Christian as archaic, anti-intellectual, and supporting dominant culture and "God and country" rhetoric.

Second, orphaned believers are spiritual orphans. The way we express our faith may look different from our parents and peers. We're stirred when cultural Christianity has usurped the gospel's call toward transformational work that leads to discomfort and disruption. Yet we remain inspired by—and live our lives centered on—the gospel story and the call of Jesus to be transformed by grace.

Some of us have experienced a double orphaning, first from church culture—reeling from -isms including nationalism, racism, and sexism. But we've also been orphaned in broader culture, where following Jesus costs social capital.

If you identify as an orphaned believer, I want to say three things. First, you're feeling this way for a reason, and it is not an accident or just in your head. Second, you have probably been feeling culturally and spiritually estranged because of specific societal and political forces that are working systemically. Third, you're far from the only one experiencing sadness, heaviness, or confusion. You are not alone.

What Has Shaped Us

I'm interested in finding what's valuable and true in complicated stories, and I believe God works in and through everything. Even every broken thing. These chapters explore how we landed at this place and what orphaned believers can do with our longing for a life formed by Jesus. We can do the work of moving forward by looking back.

I believe we can see ourselves—and our future—in a new way when we understand our common past. Considering the past helps us accept where we've come from before we move further ahead. Understanding the larger cultural and political context that shaped evangelicalism leads Christians on a clearer path toward deepened spiritual formation.

Reading accounts of evangelicalism from the '60s through the '90s and hearing stories from our friends and family of origin can't paint a whole picture of the past for us. We tend to remember history in ways that idealize or catastrophize what happened before we were born or when we were kids. The way we recall memories or are told family stories may or may not align with the reality of former events. Nostalgia can manifest itself as longing because what happened when we were younger solidified the beginning of our own spiritual formation.

But time can also make room for finding—through lines connecting the dots—how something that happened in our own lives was linked to the wider world. For example, a lot of parents in the mid-80s were concerned that backtracked vocals on records were hiding satanic messages. When no one was watching, kids like me were running our fingers counterclockwise across vinyl, trying to make out a hidden phrase. The secret message fervor had an illicit hidden treasure, cartoon-mystery vibe. We probably didn't know the reason our parents were worried about satanic messages laced into music was sparked by Senate hearings with the Parents Music Resource Council in 1985. The group worked to earmark songs in categories including "occult" on its "dirty 15" list. That throwback cultural moment is light and kitschy to most of us looking back from the 2020s, but I use it as an example of how understanding the larger context of what happened in formative years helps us make sense of trends, fears, and behaviors.

Orphaned believers are impacted by three specific failures of white American evangelicalism in the '80s and '90s that continue to shape the church today, regardless of how directly or indirectly we interacted with them: specifically, an obsession with the end times, culture wars, and consumerism.

End Times

The first area to consider how the American evangelical church failed a generation is in its discussion of the last days. You may or may not have been raised with a parent who told you Jesus would return in your lifetime, or even before you would be able to start a career or have a family. If you heard this message and carried that spiritual trauma into adulthood, it never should have happened and I'm sorry it did. You are in good company.

Your life may have been deeply impacted by fear-based end-times theology, called *premillennial dispensationalism*, or the whole "left behind" era may have been a strange curiosity, a church subculture you didn't encounter. Regardless of whether or not you have a personal end-times story to tell, dispensationalism is important to consider because it is directly tied to conspiracy theories, the rise of Donald Trump's presidency, and other power dynamics threaded through politics. Christian nationalism has irrevocably damaged American Christianity, and end-times culture is a part of the story. We are all better served by understanding how obsession with the end times in the last decades of the twentieth century still plays a role in the church and broader culture today.

Culture Wars

Second, certain cultural forces, from the New Age movement to an airport revival, from hippie Christians to modern-day miracles, shaped American religion for decades and led to a cultural estrangement for evangelicals, including many Gen Xers and Millennials.

Ironically, some Christians who entered adulthood on the more radical side of the culture of their day, as a part of the Jesus Movement, became a force for influencing conservative politics in the '80s and '90s. No culture war issue more clearly unifies and aligns American evangelicals than abortion.

When I was a teen, the emotion of abortion, the idea of a baby being murdered, landed me in a protest line, praying for young women entering into the Planned Parenthood office in my hometown. There were millions of unborn babies being killed each year, I understood, and no one counted their votes. As I moved into adulthood, like many I began to consider how few evangelicals I encountered were supporting single mothers after their babies were born or advocating for other marginalized people, including immigrants and migrant workers.

Beyond abortion, what other culture war issues paved the way for Boomers, such as my father, to hold a lifelong allegiance to the Republican Party? Christian culture wars had their own flavor in the '80s and '90s, from evolution to censorship. How did conservative politics become synonymous with evangelicalism and tarnish the witness of the church for us kids, who watched conflicts bubble up in the media and from the pulpit?

Consumerism

Third, I grew up spending Sunday morning in church and Sunday afternoon at the mall. The influence of the market on the suburban church molded my faith as much as youth group. Like a lot of peers, I moved to the city after college, leaving my suburban home. I wondered how the suburbs and consumerism meshed into the white evangelical church and how those ideals transferred to careerism, burnout, and aspirations to live in a certain bracket of lifestyle and class marked by hyper-agency and a quest for authenticity that could be both created and controlled. How did the suburbs help the church swell in size, and how did the church define the white suburban experience?

A Note to Readers

I came up in the Missional church era with a college pastor who was saved during the Jesus Movement. I have an English degree from a Midwestern Christian liberal arts college and a master's degree in nonprofit leadership from a Jesuit university. I've nearly completed coursework for a doctorate of ministry in the sacred art of writing from Western Theological Seminary. I am a member of the vestry at my local church.

I am not a historian, academic, or trained theologian. I am a writer. I am an orphaned believer—maybe like you.

I've approached *Orphaned Believers* journalistically, as is my trade, using reporting and research to uncover the cultural and political forces that landed us on this particular moment in the history of the American church. A church where, as a young Mississippi-based pastor named Skyler Flowers wrote, "the rate at which divergent views have been revealed has created jarring relational dissonance. People in the pews are left questioning the extent to which their unity is based on the Apostles or Nicene creeds or other political, cultural, and socioeconomic matters."[1] I am writing toward the central questions, How did we get here? and Where do we go?

In addition to how broader culture shapes the church and our daily lives, I'm interested in human stories. This book is as much an identity narrative as it is cultural theology.

I've also in large part written a story about a father and a daughter, which I hope brings the tenderness of generational difference to light, as well as the estrangement that can come when our politics and theology are a wide river apart from our parents'.

I began the proposal for this book the weekend before my father was diagnosed with a treatable but not curable blood cancer. The end-times theology Dad told me since I was a child was still totally plausible to him when he got sick. The many winter storm warnings, earthquakes, wars, and other current events from Y2K to 9/11 to the Arab Spring had not been bad enough to trigger the end of the world. Nor was the first red heifer born in Israel in two thousand years a sign like Dad thought it was back in 2018.[2] The blood moon and once-in-a-lifetime eclipse were also not indicators of the rapture.

Yet my father's sure-footed belief that cancer would not kill him because he would be raptured was something we talked about most weeks on the way home from chemo. I wanted to understand if my father really, truly believed he would not die from incurable cancer because he would be raptured. I share Dad's story here to illustrate how beliefs and values that are big and important to one generation can become generational trauma inherited by the next.

I am literally the child of two Boomer evangelicals. Whether or not this describes you, if you were a member of the American evangelical church in the '80s and '90s, you too are a "child" of this tradition as defined and influenced by Boomer evangelicals. No matter what generation we were born into, many of us were spiritually formed by aspects of Boomer evangelicalism, be we Gen Xers, Millennials, or members of Gen Z. We're all impacted to some degree by the same influences: Focus on the Family. See You at the Poles. Pledge allegiance to the Christian flag, then shift your gaze to pledge to the American flag. One hand over one heart. Indivisible.

I am especially interested in generational trends and am working to find the common denominator in our stories. The heart of this work is reconciliatory, and I'm ultimately working to make room for Christians to move toward—or turn back around—to Jesus. As a result, I've intended to write about the Boomer generation with care, and for nothing to land with a sharp edge of judgment or presumption.

If you are a person of color reading this book, or are in a global church context outside of Western Christianity, my hope is these chapters bring some new slant of understanding about the many ways you, as brothers and sisters in Christ, may have been met with skepticism, written off, or pushed to the sidelines by white supremacy when Christians are instead called to a kingdom of all creeds and colors worshiping Jesus. As a white American Christian, I've tried to research and write with transparency about my own culpability and continually recognize the ongoing work to surface racism in my own heart.

If you're reading this book and no longer identify as a Christian, or if you have a general curiosity about the state of the American church, I hope it will offer some context and backstory. As journalist Anne Helen Petersen wrote,

> white evangelical culture has explicitly and implicitly shaped the dominant ideologies we wade through, no matter our own belief

systems, every day. Ideals of masculinity and femininity, of course, but also of purity and nationhood, of power and dominance, of how tailgate decals . . . became commonplace in so many corners of the United States.[3]

There is an American story within this evangelical Christian story.

Reclaiming "Christian"

Finally, a note about the word *Christian*. It's important to use common and clear language to describe our belief in Jesus, and I can't find a word better than Christian. When we only define what we're estranged from, it's not enough. In the end, a sort-of Christianity falls flat, and a nostalgic Christianity becomes a memory instead of a living framework for love and restoration.

Christianity is older, larger, and more diverse than our present reality in the United States. Christianity is a big tent beyond American politics, and we are free to speak up and say "I am here." That freedom begins by reclaiming the word *Christian*. Dropping our claim of it essentially allows conspiracy theorists and white supremacists to own that real estate.

Reclaiming unifying language and reforming the church carries little lasting meaning if we do not center our lives on service. We bear witness to Christ's work in the world when we work for racial justice, equal pay for women, universal preschool, clean water, and any other systemic reform that lifts up the sidelined and brings flourishing.

As we read in James, faith without works is dead. The great joy of our faith is lifting each other up, loving each other well, and showing up for each other in the ordinary hard of life. As Mother Teresa famously said, "Not all of us can do great things. But we can do small things with great love."[4]

There's wilderness in all of us. We're lost and found a little every day. Lost or found, followers of Jesus make up the church.

The church remains our best hope. She's what Christ left us with. The church, the body of Christ, is always being reformed and renewed. Orphaned believers can reform the church, because it's the people with consciences that cry out who create change.

Many of us remain convinced Jesus wasn't only a good prophet, a historical figure, or a crucified refugee. We believe because, in the presence of our doubts, our lives have been changed and hearts softened by the gospel. Whether we're orphaned spiritually, culturally, or both, the Christian story is ours.

CHAPTER 2

Sad Confetti

Dad has cancer in his blood and bones. He says he can feel it. The doctor told us my father's cancer diagnosis plainly, like reading the weather: multiple myeloma. Receiving those words split me open. I felt like a person walking around with a giant gash from my collarbone to my stomach. Open to all bacteria and infections, every emotion moving in and out. Every feeling coming and going.

I have a young memory of watching Dad walk home from the bus after work. I am behind the screen door in our Indiana ranch at the end of the cul-de-sac. Dad is the size of a grain of rice, then a key, then an outline of himself. As he walks closer, I see that his head is surrounded by a swarm of gnats attracted to his body heat.

Treatable, Not Curable

My parents started walking in graveyards for fresh air during the Covid pandemic. Their apartment was in a dense Seattle neighborhood, and they had to drive a little way out to find less populated space. I took one "distanced" walk with them in the early weeks of Covid, months before Dad learned he was sick. First to a memorial garden with a giant Jesus statue at the edge of my neighborhood, then to a small Jewish cemetery.

Dad is easily distracted, nervous, and classic type A, and I've never been sure how he felt about slowing down to parent me. But I've not once doubted how proud he is to be Jewish. I took photos of Dad standing tall next to gravestones engraved with Stars of David. The Jewish cemetery back in his northeast Indiana hometown, where several family members are buried, is locked and gated to prevent being vandalized by anti-Semites; on one night in 2016 more than fifty headstones were pushed over or badly damaged.[1] Dad, an evangelical convert long adjusted to black sheep status in his family, says he will never be able to visit his parents' graves because the local synagogue does not welcome Messianic Jews like him. I can tell by the way he says this that part of him likes the feeling of being an outsider, and I'm fairly certain he made up that rule about not having access to his parents' graves because he converted to Christianity fifty years ago.

"I can't understand why I'm the only one who's figured this out," Dad told me, carrying groceries to his trunk after our graveyard walk. "I've been thinking that the rapture will happen this year on Pentecost." He speaks practically, like a young student solving the Pythagorean theorem in algebra. "Why don't we drive to the ocean to be raptured?" he asked me. "To be in a beautiful place."

I told him I didn't think he'd remember where he was raptured if it happened. Like when a mother forgets the pain of childbirth after the baby arrives. He was nonplussed, so I went along with his line of reasoning. "Dad, why would we drive to the Washington coast on Saturday, since Pentecost is on Sunday?" Because Israel is a day ahead, he told me, double-checking time zone math on his fingers. We'd need to consider the time change.

I knew then that I would drive with my father to Ocean Shores. Even though I didn't yet know he had cancer, I would go because he was getting older. I would go because I would regret not having the six hours in the car to hear his stories and thoughts about God, even though some of the theology attached to these beliefs has done damage to my life and Christian identity. Dad can talk anybody in or out of anything, and within five minutes it was settled. I would take the day off work and drive with him to the end of the world.

◆◆◆

Dad received his diagnosis over Labor Day weekend 2020. At that moment, time got slow and the air shifted, like when you bring a new baby home. We were closer to death than birth.

After I heard the news, I walked to the back of our yard, to a little clearing inside some greenery. I played the Sufjan Stevens song "Casimir Pulaski Day" through my headphones and cried into my sweatshirt so my kids wouldn't hear as he sang, "and he takes, and he takes, and he takes." Then I went inside and binged several episodes of a matchmaking show on Netflix.

World news had been wild all that summer. There was less reporting on war and natural disasters to put Dad on high alert in case these events signaled the rapture being close at hand. Instead, we read about protests for defunding the police, the nation reeling after the murder of George Floyd, and ballooning tallies for Covid cases. Americans were in the final months running up to the 2020 election, and it was painful to watch presidential debates. Outlandish tweets by President Trump filled our feeds. The election was on the nation's collective conscience.

◆◆◆

We talked a little bit about the presidential primaries on the way to the Washington coast, but mostly I asked Dad about converting to Christianity, his early years of marriage to my mother, and how he'd feel if the rapture happened that afternoon. We arrived three hours later and drove the car right onto the beach to park in a sandy row with other visitors.

"I'll go left, you go right," Dad said when we got out of the car. Like Abram and Lot. I didn't understand why he wouldn't choose to float up together and asked if he was sure he wanted to be alone. "I figured we're both introverts, and after the drive here from Seattle we'd want time by ourselves."

After I walked for a minute, I turned back to see him. I kept pacing backward on the sand, watching, until my father was an outline of himself. Then a key. Then a grain of rice. Sand flies picked apart a washed-up crab at my feet. A constellation of cancer.

It was a sunny, windy day, and the Pacific was choppy. Someone had brought a pet potbellied pig to shuffle down the shore. A dozen people were riding horses. I saw a young father and his toddler running for the waves, near two seagulls diving for fish. I didn't grow up with a day-at-the-beach dad; we rarely spent time outdoors as a family. Most vacations were to New York City or Chicago, to a place that matched Dad's pace.

Geoducks bubbled up water in pockets in the sand. "Lord," I prayed, "let a little bit of life spring up in me."

We drove to the end of the world, and we met up back at the car twenty minutes later.

While we traveled to the coast, Dad carried nervous energy for what could happen. But we did not float up. We did not feel how Jesus felt ascending to heaven while the disciples were left with the hovering flame. Our newly whole and perfect bodies did not rise higher than the snowy Olympics, to be capped by a cloud.

Our drive back to the city was quiet. We stopped at Dairy Queen for a cherry Mister Misty on the way, like when I was a kid. We made it home in no time, the pandemic having lightened traffic. On a near-empty interstate, we drove past the closed Tacoma Mall parking lot, toward Seattle's vacant downtown with street lights on and office lights out.

A few weeks later, my husband, kids, and I hosted Mom and Dad in the backyard for a socially distanced Father's Day barbecue. Our family hadn't hugged my parents for months for fear of Covid. But after dinner, Dad asked me to cut his hair.

I did terribly and ended up buzzing it because of how I'd botched it. But on the lawn chair, in the grass, I touched Dad's head as I shaved the back of his neck. He was a little tan and had powdered sugar on his shirt from beignets.

The lesions were already on his skull then, and dotting his rib cage, spine, and both hip bones. He would become covered with them—sad confetti. Today they are smeared across his skeleton like hydrogenated birthday cake frosting.

Late Great

Like Dad, the early church believed Jesus was coming back in their lifetime. Christ followers in the book of Acts were radical, with a fresh faith that was catching on and multiplying. But they were also logical. Some in the group of earliest Christians had witnessed Jesus ascend until he was a dot in the sky. Naturally, nothing would be more rational than a round-trip ticket.

The expectation of the Jewish Messiah was for a king. But Jesus died and never established a kingdom. In order for Jesus to complete his work as Messiah, he had to fully establish his realm on earth as it is in heaven. The orthodox understanding of the second coming of Jesus is that one day, Jesus will answer everything, make everything right, judge all powers and rulers, and finally establish a forever kingdom. And like the early church, we're still waiting for his return and restorative, eternal reign.

The Christian posture of having our eyes open to the return of Jesus has always been a thread in church history: orthodox interpretations of prophetic literature center on the idea that believers will see Christ return. Progressive Christians in liberal Protestant traditions who interpret the return of Jesus as allegorical are also optimistic that followers of Christ are part of something special: that believers will see, if not a bodily return of Jesus, a greater culture shift back to the church.

Along with millions of other evangelicals of his era, Dad learned about the second coming of Jesus after reading Hal Lindsey's (and writer Carole C. Carlson's) book *The Late Great Planet Earth*.[2] When Zondervan published *Late Great* in 1970, the United States was still in the middle of the Vietnam War. Student protestors were shot dead by the National Guard at Kent State that year. Martin Luther King Jr. had been assassinated two years prior, and a generation of young people were in the middle of political, racial, and social reckonings.

Late Great sold ten million copies in the '70s and landed at the top of the *New York Times* bestsellers list, where it hovered for the entire decade; *Your Erogenous Zones* and *The Joy of Sex* came in third and fourth place.[3] By the end of the decade, *Late Great* had been translated into several languages. More than pleasure, in the '70s, Americans were reading about fear.

A few years later a prime-time, made-for-TV special of *Late Great Planet Earth* narrated by Orson Welles flickered across millions of American television screens. The *New York Times* movie review put it this way: "Well, our goose is cooked." The film was rated PG for "moderate gruesome newsreel shots of war being waged, and one brief scene featuring the Whore of Babylon."[4]

American politics also mingled with end-times buzzwords. In 1984, for example, Ronald Reagan was criticized by mainstream clergy of evoking fear of a nuclear battle with Russia by weaving the word *Armageddon* into his talking points during the Cold War.[5]

Tom and Sue

Dad met Mom in 1969, a year before he would read *The Late Great Planet Earth*. He was a teenager, driving with a friend from Fort Wayne, Indiana, to a tavern in Celina, Ohio, near the Indiana border. The legal drinking age was twenty-one in Indiana, but eighteen-year-olds could drink beer in Ohio until the mid-80s, when the National Minimum Drinking Age Act was passed by Congress. A lot of Indiana kids would drive out to Ohio taverns on the weekend.

That's where Dad first saw Mom, a Chicago-raised Italian who'd recently moved to Fort Wayne with her parents. In a story I've heard

Dad tell countless times over the years, he was in the bar and followed a perfume scent that led him to Mom. "I'm Tom; my father is a prominent Fort Wayne dentist," he told her. "I don't care who your father is," Mom snapped back. Dad convinced her friend to give him Mom's number.

They quickly married and moved into a little apartment in downtown Fort Wayne above the St. Marys River, but they separated after six months. Mom came home and found a note on the dining room table: "Sue: I want a divorce. Call my brother, who is now my attorney." What happened next looked like the beginning of a romantic dramedy. She threw all his things off the balcony, packed up her black Ford Maverick, and, sobbing, drove back to Chicago. I imagine Dad's umbrella, loafers, and portable radio floating downstream in the cloudy river water.

After Mom and Dad had been divorced for a few months, Dad said he "got desperate" and accepted an invitation from a friend to attend a Bible study with other young people. The group was studying the Old Testament book of Daniel. After a few meetings, he said, a light bulb flicked on. His heart started to burn. The movie continues in my mind. Dad said he leaped over a sofa like a high-jumper and ran outside, fell on his knees in the parking lot, and prayed the sinner's prayer.

At that moment, my father became a Jewish Christian.

Several of my father's friends, some of whom he met at the Bible study that led to his conversion, had been to Vietnam. All had come of age during the turbulent '60s. By the time I was a kid in the '80s, nuclear families like ours had moved to the suburbs, and none of us kids cared if Mom had worn tie-dye in college.

Many of Dad's evangelical peers from the '70s have remained loyal friends to my parents all these decades later, sending practical and emotional support from across the country after Dad's myeloma diagnosis.

After two weeks in a Seattle hospital, Dad's failing kidneys were salvaged, and he had completed a first round of chemo. No one could visit because of Covid restrictions, and we were unprepared for how he looked when he was discharged in mid-September.

◆◆◆

I picked him up from the twelfth floor of the hospital ward, where I imagined the most serious patients went, since it had the best views of Mt. Rainier. When I walked in the room, I saw my father, sleeping sitting up in a chair near the window. His stomach was distended and his arms bruised from chemo shots and blood draws, and oh my God. When he woke, I saw his eyes had changed.

Mom noticed too and said they reminded her of when she saw him for the first time after he was saved. In another rom-com scene, they remarried in 1974, saying vows in front of a priest, a rabbi, and a minister to appease Catholic, Jewish, and evangelical family and friends.

Now I saw it: in the hospital, his body was weak and his eyes were lit up. His pupils were very small, and he stared, without irony, for a little too long. His eyes were like neon jellyfish stingers in murky waters and just as beautiful. "Do you know your eyes look different now?" I asked him. "Piercing?"

"Even without looking I know," he said.

While we waited for his discharge papers, I asked Dad if he still believed the rapture was going to happen in his lifetime, with a cancer diagnosis that was treatable but not curable. His genetics and staging predicted a three-and-a-half-year survival rate.

"Do you really want me to tell you?" he asked. I told him, of course, lay it on me. "I'm even more sure of it," he said. I felt deflated but not surprised. I understood something in his response, considering my own stubborn beliefs and anxious tendencies that I often soothe with a wandering imagination.

Then I asked him—nervously, to be honest. "Did you like being a dad?"

My heart leaped when he stared at me for a long time before speaking. "I adored it."

Stockholm Syndrome

When do bad theology and frenzied faith become spiritual abuse? Is there a clear line, or a survey score to tell us the difference between misguidance and harm?

Spiritual abuse is ubiquitous with other forms of emotional and psychological injury inflicted by another. Even WebMD has a definition: "Any attempt to exert power and control over someone using religion, faith, or beliefs can be spiritual abuse. Spiritual abuse can happen within a religious organization or a personal relationship."[6]

The things Dad taught me about the end times clouded my thoughts. He turned my posture toward fear and away from joy and peace. Did Dad, intentionally or inadvertently, attempt to control me by using fear of the world ending? Did he try to drag me kicking and screaming into the kingdom? Because I went along willingly, and I took the sweet parts of following Jesus with the fear of Jesus returning before I could begin an independent life.

Dad, in my adulthood, has told me he regrets raising me steeped in fear of the world ending. His face washes with red guilt when he apologizes for how he talked about the rapture as an inevitability. He has apologized so much I wonder if it's more for me or for him. I forgave him a long time ago.

There's another particular way in which my father's identity is woven into his beliefs about the end times. For many people in his life, each quip about the battle of Gog and Magog or the rapture is received as another "Oh, that's just Tom." It's just a quirky part of him, friends who are not dispensationalists say. At points, even to me, Dad's full allegiance to the coming rapture is absurdly lovable.

Anyone who meets my father either loves him or keeps their distance. Approximately 75 percent love him. They did not grow up with him. Before cancer, he was cranky, up and down all night. In my small childhood home, I would listen, half-awake, as he shuffled to the kitchen for his midnight snack of celery cold out of the fridge.

In the morning, I'd find the tub of Philadelphia cream cheese on the counter with stab marks from the stalks.

Dad stocks up on ChapStick, nail clippers, and individual Kleenex packets. He asks for extra napkins at each restaurant meal. He orders you a large when you ask for a small.

He is not sure if his own mother loved or even liked him, which is both a true possibility and very sad. When I was eight and he was almost forty, Dad ordered chocolate milk at Peaches, the brunch-in-a-hotel place where they made custom waffles for guests and served '80s fancy food like frog legs. My grandmother, sitting across the table, began to publicly shame him, walking up to neighboring tables and telling them, "Would you believe my son? A grown man, at a place like this, ordering chocolate milk." After a few minutes Mom stood up and yelled, "Tom, Sara, come on. We're leaving." I leaped up, stomped a foot in protest, and nodded my head toward my grandmother, shouting, "Yeah!"

Dad is also exceedingly forgiving and would do anything for anybody if it helps. He eats meat, potatoes, and fruit-flavored candy. During the early months of Covid, when I shopped for my parents, he wrote grocery lists including the following: "2 boxes of KRAFT ONLY macaroni and cheese original flavor please make sure it is not the kid shape but has the shape of a noodle the box is deceptive so do not be fooled."

I have, at times, with full earnestness, considered my father my best friend. Is that some kind of paternal Stockholm Syndrome? Have I sided with the person who brought fear into my beliefs? I know this for certain: I've sided with my wounded, wounding father.

◆◆◆

It was clear and sunny when I picked Dad up from the hospital after he was discharged. As we drove to his apartment, he kept saying things like, "The flowers are so beautiful," and, "Look at that color. I've never noticed it before." He was like a kid seeing the ocean or

Mt. Rainier for the first time. Everything was vivid and majestic, and I saw it too.

"Don't you wonder who you'll be without your dad?" my spiritual director, Shelly, asked after he got sick. I'd called her from my yoga mat, trying to work out in my muscles what I could not work out in my head and heart. "You can't change him," she said. "So just love him while he's here."

My dad will die, and when he does, I will probably be alive. I will live without my dad, but I do not know who I'll be without him. After I hung up with Shelly I stretched across the mat. *I don't know who I will be when he is gone*, I repeated to myself, moving into some contortion of child's pose.

CHAPTER 3

End-Times Kids

The school bus swerving off the road without a driver, the empty bank teller booth, the vacant drive-thru window with fries getting cold while cars wait in line. The images are clear in my mind even now, well past the decades I believed the end of the world would soon arrive.

By the time I was in middle school, I knew the rapture was real and coming at any moment with as much assurance as I knew the Twin Towers were real and not just buildings I'd seen in photographs. I walked up and touched the base of the South Tower during a trip from Indiana to Manhattan when I turned eleven. Dad and I then took the elevator to the 107th floor, called the Top of the World. I looked down at the nighttime street, forehead pressed against the cold glass. I was a Christian, and when Jesus returned, I was going to fly.

Strange and Unusual

In my family, we talked about the end of the world at dinner like some people talk about football. The end times were a sport.

I thought I was the only kid who grew up believing Jesus would return before I could pass through life milestones like graduating high school or experiencing motherhood. I later learned several evangelical friends had the same fears of the rapture when they were growing up. We share the common experience of our parents or pastor explaining that the world would almost certainly end in our lifetime. Like 9/11, we can tell you where we were and how we felt when we were first told. My husband was a third grader lying in the back seat of his car near Baltimore when his dad told him about the rapture. He remembers wiping away hot tears from fear that he wouldn't get to grow up.

This stuff is weird! It was weird when I heard about it as a kid, and it's equally strange and unusual when I think about it now. I imagine folk artist renderings of the creature with ten horns that fall off to reveal a more terrifying one. I imagine the twelve gem layers of the new Jerusalem like a wobbly twelve-layer gelatin mold. Images in the book of Revelation are extraordinary and terrifying. The sword in the mouth of Jesus. The whore of Babylon. The vampiric Antichrist.

With *Late Great*'s guidance, Dad and many of his evangelical peers accepted that the rapture was coming in their lifetime. Lindsey's message especially resonated with hippie Christians in Dad's Boomer generation, many of whom were hungry for more casual iterations of Protestantism that diverged from starchy Sunday services.

My father was more interested in eating frozen Snickers bars by the pool and looking for dates than participating in protests or having an opinion about politics or anti-war sentiment central to hippie culture. Loosely raised in the Reformed Jewish tradition, Dad tended to avoid going to temple on Shabbat. After his conversion to Christianity, he also wanted to avoid stodgy sermons, hard wooden pews, and dusty hymns in the churches his new evangelical friends' parents attended. But like the hippie kids he saw hanging around downtown, Dad "longed for ideas—Christian or otherwise—that bucked conventional wisdom of their suburban upbringing."[1] Dispensationalism let Dad find a burgeoning subculture in evangelicalism that began to grow one hundred years before *Late Great* was published.

Premillennial Dispensationalism

While there have always been Christians fixated on apocalyptic writing and prophecy, Anglo-Irish Plymouth Brethren minister John Nelson Darby is considered the founding father of dispensationalism—the idea that biblical history can be separated into seven distinct periods, called "dispensations." American theologian C. I. Scofield later defined the eras into seven distinct ages, including "Innocency," the time before the fall, "Conscience," the period from the fall to the flood, and so on, from Moses to Jesus to the church age and coming millennium.[2]

While the word *rapture* is not included in the Old or New Testament, Darby popularized it. Matthew Avery Sutton writes in *American Apocalypse: A History of Modern Evangelicalism*, "Identifying and explaining the rapture—a dramatic experience in which all living Christians will mysteriously vanish from the earth and the dead will rise to heaven—was one of Darby's great theological innovations."[3]

Along with rejecting church hierarchy and denominations, Darby taught that the second coming of Jesus would begin (and Christians would be raptured) before a thousand-year reign of Christ, a belief called premillennial dispensationalism.[4] Centering on Israel's role in the end times is a distinctive characteristic of this teaching.[5] The restoration of Israel would be a key sign the end times had started, an idea that laid the groundwork for Christian Zionism. For some members of the Messianic Jewish community like Dad, a focus on the rebuilding of the temple and the restoration of Israel made the theology especially compelling.

Millions of kids of evangelical Boomers like me experienced a particular flavor of rapture anxiety dramatized on screen during youth group lock-ins and on the pages of the Left Behind series of novels. We knew the script: after the rapture, most dispensationalists believe that a seven-year tribulation begins. The Antichrist gains power cloaked as a harbinger of peace for seven years. At the end of those years, Jesus returns to overcome the Antichrist in a battle, and the final thousand-year dispensation begins before a new heaven and new earth are established.

Before Darby's influence in the mid-1800s, postmillennialism—the belief that Jesus will return after a thousand years of peace—was a common apocalyptic view. Postmillennial theology complemented the work of Christians who were reforming and seeking to improve the world in those decades, essentially making it better ahead of the return of Christ.

Instead of focusing on a dismal future, the American church's postmillennial theology during the early- to mid-nineteenth century gave shape to vigorous engagement around social causes. This optimistic view of the future led to an empowerment of Christians who believed they could confront social challenges of their time—including child labor laws, women's voting rights, and the abolition of slavery—and create a brighter future. Postmillennialism held that Jesus would return after a thousand years, be it literal or figurative, as God's kingdom would slowly grow and spread. Shaped by an optimistic eschatology, followers of this activist expression of Christianity believed it could move the church closer to a golden era that would usher in the return of Jesus.

But Darby's premillennial dispensationalism spread from Ireland to Europe to America, gradually replacing postmillennialism in the United States after the Civil War ended. Following Darby's death in 1882, a subset of pastors across the states began to popularize his message, including William B. Riley and Aimee Semple McPherson.[6]

Premillennial dispensationalism began to catch on at the same time an influx of immigrants including European Catholics and Jews changed the face of American cities, shifting demographics. Like today, some white Anglo-Saxon Protestants felt threatened by diversification. Premillennialism was a sweet escape from the feeling that the world was changing and out of control, and an ideological home for the frenetic energy of an evolving population fresh from a bloody war.[7] It continued to spread during World War I. The "Great

War" with its industrialized bloodshed made an impending end of days seem self-evident. Plus, current events in the early 1900s, including the rise of Darwinism and the Scopes Monkey Trial in the 1920s, were signals to some dispensationalists that the return of Christ was imminent.[8]

JC Light and Power House Roots

Fifty years later, Lindsey's *Late Great Planet Earth* continued to popularize dispensationalism with a fresh twist that engaged readers like Dad.

Hal Lindsey was a Youth for Christ staffer in the Bay Area before *Late Great* was published. He launched a dormitory for about forty students called JC Light and Power House in an old frat house at UCLA in 1969.[9] Here, Lindsey charged a nominal fee for a class "in which [he] expounded on the narrative of geopolitical apocalypse" and honed his skills for presenting a big message in a digestible way that resonated with young people.[10]

Using a tone that caught on because it read as anti-establishment and conversational, Lindsey explained signs to watch for before Christ's return, like the rebuilding of the Jewish temple in Jerusalem. He also called out two key historical events that had already occurred: the establishment of Israel in 1948 and the Jewish victory in the 1967 Arab-Israeli War, which gave Jews jurisdiction over holy sites. An increase in natural disasters and the rise of communism were additional guideposts confirming the impending return of Jesus. The Russian nuclear threat is woven into Lindsey's message, which made *Late Great*'s message especially resonant during the Cold War.

Because it was only sold in religious bookstores and through the mail under the Zondervan moniker, *Late Great* didn't appear on the *New York Times* bestsellers list after its initial release. Instead, the book cultivated the luster of outsider status, perhaps adding to its aura of credibility among a growing and loyal readership. A later mass-market edition was distributed by Bantam, and the book began its climb as a bestseller.[11] As one critic noted, "only the Bible itself had outsold *The Late Great Planet Earth*."[12] *Late Great* crossed over to mainstream publishing with ease, likely because of its low-brow, "folksy" tone.

Unsurprisingly, Lindsey was not received warmly by secular media, who were quick to note the worldly benefits of bestseller status. A 1977 *Publishers Weekly* piece was especially biting:

> Hal Lindsey . . . is an Advent-and-Apocalypse evangelist who sports a Porsche racing jacket and tools around Los Angeles in a Mercedes. . . . And even though his best-selling books of Bible prophecy warn that the end is near, Lindsey maintains a suite of offices in a posh Santa Monica high-rise for the personal management firm that sinks his royalties into long-term real estate investments.[13]

Luring Escapism

For Dad and other evangelicals who kept *Late Great* close to their Bibles, the threat of the enemy—and of impending desolation—became personified through end-times culture.

Some Christians were drawn to the rapture narrative to cope with life being, well, scary. There was a luring sense of escapism ingrained in the evangelical consciousness around premillennial theology, a thread that continues into today. End-times culture swelled in a volatile time in American history, and although it may not sound logical, the rapture brought emotional comfort to certain evangelicals. If a person believed the rapture would happen in their lifetime, the pain and suffering inflicted by the Antichrist's rule could be averted. A near future in heaven that escaped war and political unrest—and sidestepped bodily sickness and death—awaited.

Young people in the '70s who were attracted to the rapture narrative had endured their fair share of difficulty. It was a time of economic insecurity and cultural change, including the end of the Vietnam War, Nixon's impeachment, the nuclear arms race, and stagflation. It was also an anxious time, and Lindsey couldn't have picked a sweeter low-hanging fruit to feed a skittish population of white evangelicals. Plus, it offered Christians like Dad a community of peers who read the same books, listened to the same music, and thought through the same ideas together.

Gorbachev's Birthmark

Dinner table speculations about the possible identity of the Antichrist were common throughout my childhood. He was certainly a man and not a woman, Dad said, because he would be a mock Jesus and Jesus was male. Dad also said some people thought he could have been Nero or Rockefeller, but then they both died. Maybe he was Bill Clinton.

But based on an interpretation of Daniel's dream of King Nebuchadnezzar in Daniel 2 (and his later dream about a beast with ten horns in Daniel 7), many modern dispensationalists deduced that the Antichrist would likely hail from the European Union. That prediction mirrored Roman rule in the time of Jesus. In a savage twist, this makes the pope—whoever happens to be the current one—a likely culprit. Questioning whether or not the pope, any pope, is the Antichrist links with a long history. From the start of the Reformation, Protestants motivated by anti-Catholic sentiment have been calling the pope the Antichrist.[14]

Projections of the Antichrist's identity have been even wilder than that, including a stretch in the 1980s when a theory gained momentum that it was Soviet Union president Mikhail Gorbachev. A popular dispensationalist view holds that the Antichrist will be shot after reigning for three-and-a-half years during the seven-year tribulation period. Gorbachev had an unmistakable red birthmark on his head, leading some to believe the birthmark was an early warning.

"When I look at the top of Gorbachev's head, I see a red dragon and over the right eye, there's a tail that hangs, representing stars," author and numerologist Robert W. Faid told the *Washington Post* in 1988.[15]

We didn't know who the Antichrist was, exactly, but the point Dad drove home was that he was a real literal person, living and breathing, and almost certainly alive at that time. When Dad would go through his mental Rolodex of who the Antichrist might be, I would think of *Rosemary's Baby*, which I watched at much too young an age. In one infamous scene, Mia Farrow's character is pregnant with the Antichrist and craves raw meat. The camera catches her in the kitchen, feasting.

These days, whoever the Antichrist will turn out to be, Dad is sure he (a) is not Mikhail Gorbachev and (b) will be shot and killed in the middle of the tribulation period. After that, Dad's interpretation of the seven-year-period becomes a little fuzzier. The Antichrist may be brought back from the dead by the devil, as some dispensationalists conjecture. Or maybe the devil will just make everyone think so. Dad says either way, after the Antichrist is shot he will in some form set up a statue of himself in the rebuilt temple. Every person will be made to worship this statue as a part of the "abomination and desolation" referenced in Daniel 9 and 11. Like a mock resurrection. If anyone doesn't bow down to the statue and take the mark of the beast, they will be killed.

Whenever this topic comes up with Dad, I still think of the guillotine scene in 1978's *A Distant Thunder*, where Christians choose to be beheaded rather than take the mark of the beast on their hand or forehead. I saw this Christian scare film before my tenth birthday. It includes a flashback to when the film's heroine visited her grandmother, who was raptured while she was left behind. While baking gingerbread cookies in a checkered apron, Granny tells her unsaved granddaughter to read from Revelation 13. She then explains what the world will be like for those who did not accept Jesus, and how many will take the mark of the beast. "To a lot of people, it will seem like a new type of credit card," Granny says, "and people will welcome it."[16]

A Distant Thunder is the second in a trilogy of movies that started with 1972's *A Thief in the Night.* These films were viewed in youth groups and living rooms across the country. They were evangelical kids' versions of scary stories around the campfire.

Anti-Christ, Pro-Literalism

Dad holds a "literal interpretation" of the Bible, including the book of Revelation. By "literal" he means *selectively* literal. Jesus's parables are parables, sure, but Dad "reads it plain." Symbol and allegory do not hold assurance when it comes to biblical prophecy.

As members of my generation who heard these messages moved into adulthood, started having children, and settled into careers we were told would never happen, it's natural that many of us have questioned such "literal" interpretations of the end times.

While my own reading of the book of Revelation is now allegorical, many Christians, including Boomer evangelicals, maintain a premillennial dispensationalist interpretation of the end times. A 2010 Pew survey found that 58 percent of white American evangelicals from all age groups surveyed believe that Jesus will either probably or definitely return by the year 2050.[17] That's in contrast to 32 percent of Catholic respondents.

Beyond "literal," most sentiment around the apocalypse is Western. It's common for Gen Xers and Millennials to have family members who fought in or protested the conflict in Vietnam. Many also had grandparents who saw combat in the Korean War or World War II.

While our parents and grandparents did not witness war on American soil, they felt its impending weight. They may have grappled with the idea that at any moment, Soviet Premier Khrushchev could push a button and detonate a nuclear weapon.

Millions of American families watched President Kennedy address the nation in October 1962 during the Cuban Missile Crisis. "We no longer live in a world where only the actual firing of weapons represents a sufficient challenge to a nation's security to constitute maximum peril," Kennedy said. "Nuclear weapons are so destructive and ballistic missiles are so swift, that any substantially increased possibility of their use or any sudden change in their deployment may well be regarded as a definite threat to peace."[18]

American Boomers and members of the Greatest Generation did not fear the world ending because a war was literally happening outside their doors. They were not survivors of the Bangladesh Liberation War or caught up in the Iran-Contra like Nicaraguan families.

Yet the impending nuclear threat, the end of their world, was palpable. The year before, President Kennedy encouraged Americans to build backyard bomb shelters, and Congress earmarked $169 million to construct fallout shelters.[19] An estimated two hundred thousand private shelters were built in homes by 1965.[20] In school, Boomers practiced duck-and-cover drills under their desks in preparation for a nuclear attack like kids today practice shelter-in-place drills for active shooters.

Black Eschatology

Today the Black church carries the torch of the social gospel in many issues, including police reform, health care, food security, and a call for reparations. Similar issues of the day were once center points of white postmillennial evangelicals, who were active in social justice work in the early 1900s. But as Darby's dispensationalism took root, a key timeline shifted, and with it a focus from the collective to the individual.

Dispensationalism adhered to by white evangelicals was motivated at least in part by a search for personal salvation and security. There was also an aspect of whiteness infused in this end-times culture. Georgetown professor Charles King recounts his dispensationalist upbringing in *Time*.

We knew a few Italian Catholics, had heard of Jews (misguided, we believed, but mysteriously favored by God), and might have spoken once or twice to a Black person from a neighboring town. But we assumed that when Christ returned and set up his kingdom, people like us—white and righteous—would be first in line at his heavenly palace.[21]

To contrast the individual focus of white dispensationalism, Black eschatology is, in the words of Wake Forest divinity professor and African American scholar Derek S. Hicks, community-based eschatology. "African Americans are only partially served by an eschatology connected to evangelical ideas of future eternal reward in Christ based on saving faith," Hicks writes.

> For them, a component that identifies the needs and values of the community must also affect any eschatology . . . eschatological analysis must also be grounded in the historical present, and must challenge present circumstances that stand in contrast to God's desire for justice and equality for all people.[22]

Hicks goes on to highlight a speech by Martin Luther King Jr., delivered the evening before he was assassinated. King said,

> It's all right to talk about "streets flowing with milk and honey," but God has commanded us to be concerned about the slums down here, and his children who can't eat three square meals a day. It's all right to talk about the new Jerusalem, but one day, God's preacher must talk about the new New York, the new Atlanta, the new Philadelphia, the new Los Angeles, the new Memphis, Tennessee. This is what we have to do.[23]

Here, future hope is collective hope, and redemption is rooted in social justice and community transformation.

Before or After

A lot hinges on whether the thousand-year rule of Christ comes before or after the rapture. That timeline is a defining differentiator between pre- and postmillennialists. Because if the thousand-year rule of Christ occurs before the rapture, as postmillennialists hold, it means Christians are here for the pain and suffering too.

In addition to systemic impact, there are environmental implications to dispensationalism. Environmentalism was generally deprioritized in the dispensationalist worldview I was taught. If Christians weren't going to be around after the rapture, and it was literally coming soon, there was little motivation for fighting climate change. This line of thinking led me to be skeptical of Earth Day throughout my youth.

For dispensationalists like Dad, a tangible benefit is the reassurance that believers can circumvent apocalyptic trauma. The draw of dispensationalism is the unspoken message that Christians might not get a pass for an affliction-free life before the rapture, but at least we could skip suffering through an apocalypse. And if America could scoot out of the Cold War without getting ourselves obliterated, we can also float up before the guillotines and marks of the beast.

Well into my teen years, I carried a sense of melodramatic exceptionalism I picked up from my dispensationalist parents and their friends. Conversely, I mourned for friends and extended family who I believed would not be raptured. I remember throwing myself in the back seat, sobbing, when I tried and failed to convert my Catholic grandfather to evangelicalism and was certain he was going to hell. The intention was tender but the theology misguided.

We long for people we love to float up. We pray and plead. But when it comes to the masses, the faceless everybody else, I intuited that it would be easier to be raptured than bear the world's burdens. That deep down, most of us would pick the less painful path.

Still, as a high school student, I felt it was my duty to reveal the coming rapture to my friends, so there was some possibility of fewer people remaining on earth after Jesus returned.

Sitting in the back booth of Scoops ice cream parlor sophomore year, I told my friend how the end of the world would go down while we were eating banana splits. I can clearly remember the way she looked at me, spoon suspended midbite and mouth open, when I spoke with confidence about the thousand-year age of peace before the final battle of Gog and Magog.

#raptureanxiety

Tweets using the hashtag #raptureanxiety surfaced in the late 2010s. This was around the time President Trump called for the American embassy to be moved to Jerusalem, a key location in some dispensationalist readings of Revelation.[24]

You could spend hours scrolling through #raptureanxiety threads on Twitter. Sometimes these stories are told in a way that is campy and colorful. Kind of eye-rolly. Melodramatic and cinematic. Other times they are heartbreaking. Often they're both.

My friend Dan collected twenty interviews about end-times trauma as a part of a podcast series that included stories recollecting how kids lived in fear of the world ending.[25] I found these stories wrenchingly relatable and sad. Many recount a certain moment when they were sure the rapture was on the cusp, just over the horizon.

My spiritual director walked outside one evening when she was a teenager to see a blood red sky and was sure the world was about to end. When my pastor was a teenager in the '80s, he watched a woman stand on a chair at a neighboring table in a pizza place and shout repeatedly, "Ronald Reagan is the Antichrist!" There is little that is funny or ironic about these disarming moments at the time they are experienced. They are often burned into our minds.

I spoke with one woman who had the wherewithal to shrug off eschatological messages about the world ending. She never took her parents' or pastor's end-times theology especially seriously. But for many, experiences of rapture anxiety are deep and ingrained, because they happened during youth, when identity begins to solidify.

Ironically, our parents may have been drawn to *Late Great* because they were searching for belonging. A National Endowment for the Humanities feature on *Late Great* put it this way:

> While texts like *The Late Great Planet Earth* had implications for nuclear nonproliferation and foreign policy, they also had an impact on miserable kids who desperately wanted out of their suffocating high school worlds. Young men whose countercultural girlfriends were into both Jesus and New Age stuff, and people who wanted to fit into church youth groups where *The Late Great Planet Earth* had replaced the Bible.[26]

The rapture narrative plays on the way we are wired to seek control. When you know something you think others don't, self-aggrandizement can quickly follow. Dad believed that preparing me for the rapture was a sort of spiritual inoculation. When he talked to me about the end times as a kid, he thought he was telling it to me straight. That once I got over the shock I could join with him in the excitement.

Besides fear, the truth is I did also experience a small swell of excitement when Dad talked about the end times. We were in on something big, and we knew the signs like a doctor who could spot the early onset of a disease. I was told that more earthquakes and floods were not the result of climate change but a fulfillment of biblical prophecy. For Dad, even the falling of the Berlin Wall was a sign of change that could point to a greater story God was writing about power shifting hands in the last days.

As a kid, every news report of a war, famine, or tsunami became another piece of evidence that the end times were truly upon us. While I joined the other kids in eating multiple bowls of cereal in front of Saturday cartoons or taking turns on the Slip 'n' Slide, I also spent time playing a sad game in my head I didn't dare talk about. I would close my eyes and think, *Jesus is returning . . . now!* Nothing happened. *Now! . . . Now!*

Maybe this impulse to predict the future stems from a distorted desire in some for our personal lives to unfold during monumental change. Change that can be expected and can therefore be controlled.

Until, one day, we stop waiting and realize the second coming is a great and good mystery. Because if no one truly knows the day or hour, we can finally stop guessing and focus on living.

6-6-6

About a year after we drove to the coast to wait for the rapture, Dad emailed me an apology for that end of the world beach trip. It was summer 2021 and his cancer was in remission. He was his usual mix of sweet, funny, and guilty. He was still convinced he would see Jesus return with his own eyes. Dad was a victim of his end-times beliefs too. I wondered how let down he felt when Y2K melted into January 2000, and how he felt every Jewish New Year when Jesus did not return as he'd hoped.

His thoughts and time have been taken up with rapture obsessions and ruminations. He has listened to the bad math of fringe pastors he hoped would offer a new slant on end-times interpretations. If he has felt a burn of embarrassment or shame, he has never spoken of it. If he has experienced end-times trauma of his own, he does not have the language for it. He has shaken off disappointment and kept his gaze ahead.

Except when it came to the way he raised me. "I was such a fool to put this heavy burden on you at such a young age and for that I deeply am sorry," he wrote in the email.

> I consider myself part of the remnant church made up of mostly old codgers that follow this eschatological view from just a few pastors that tell us that we are no longer in the last days but even in the last hours of the last days before the rapture. The bottom line is that we both will one day spend our eternity with our Blessed Hope and that is the sweetest thing of all.

Decades before this apology email and well before I could recite an apocalyptic timeline to friends in high school, fear of the end times took root when I was a small child. It is still in me as I type; I can feel a slight grip, a thread of old-time fear.

When I was six, I traced 6-6-6 on my forehead with my pointer finger. I'd heard Dad talk about the mark of the beast and knew that anyone who accepted it on their forehead or arm would be cut off from the promise of heaven. Then I ran to my mom in the yard and burst into tears. "Mom! I'm going to hell!" I wallowed. She hugged me for a long time until the fear that gripped me—moments of temporary paralysis after a nightmare—softened.

It would be years before God would unstick my fearful heart and bring me to a spacious place.

True Apocalypse

End-times theology popularized by books including *The Late Great Planet Earth* and Christian scare films in the '70s and early '80s were an escape for millions of people. A thrill of hope. For some, it was trauma that lasted for decades and is carried to this day. For others it was scary but blockbuster-worthy. A freaky feeling you shake off after you leave the theatre and go to an all-night diner for a plate of tan-colored food until the movie's creepiness begins to lift.

The Hollywoodification of rapture anxiety has accomplished two things. First, for Christians, the industry built around *Late Great* and *Left Behind*–era end-times media spiked both fear and profit, because fear sells and makes good stories. Stories that center true believers as wise heroes given knowledge to overcome damnation while most of the world reels. Second, for people who don't identify as Christians, rapture culture is characterized by a lampooned, wacky set of missed predictions for the return of Jesus that has become the butt of jokes matched in number with the bobblehead Jesus figurines lining joke shop shelves.

However, on-screen portrayals about the end times have seeped into popular culture and created a new, gnarly beast. The cultural idea of apocalypse has now become synonymous with an earth-ending event alongside cataclysmic asteroids, nuclear bombs, and aliens.

For some Christians coming up in the '60s and '70s, emerging out of difficult decades, the rapture narrative was hopeful in the way believing the same things your friends believe brings comfort with community. But their kids, and many people of all ages, received end-times messages in different ways.

Some of us have been grounded enough to shake them off. But even if we missed personal trauma, all American Christians are caught in the wake of rapture anxiety because it impacts politics and culture in broad strokes.

Yet no matter how little or gaping the wound, how scarred over or fresh, there is a way toward healthy hope for Jesus's return, rooted in historic Christianity. For those of us who have carried anxiety about the end of the world from our earliest years, a balm comes when we understand that true apocalypse is an unveiling. An apocalypse is not a catastrophe or an end. Instead, it is a way to uncover what is true. To reveal. Our uncovering is an apocalypse.

A great reclamation of the word comes when we use it as a tool to surface what needs to be *undone*. There are wrongs that should come to light, that should be surfaced—for example, abuse of power from church leaders, and the conflation of evangelicalism and Republicanism. In that sense, our healing can be born from a right view of apocalypse.

The Covid pandemic was apocalyptic because it exposed to many of us what values and priorities motivate our finite lives.[27] What matters to us surfaced in the pandemic years—a reaction between the heart and the spirit. Baking soda and vinegar.

A disastrous consequence of end-times culture is the potential for a premillennial dispensationalist to lose—or fully abdicate—personal agency and individual responsibility. In its worst distortion, waiting for the rapture removes motivation for direct service. Leave the city, move to an area where it is safe for white families. Maybe return to the old neighborhood a couple of decades later, riding a wave of gentrification. But expending extra energy on recycling waste or community engagement is not needed when the rapture alleviates the desire to improve. Whether fueled by end-times culture or by generalized anxiety, white middle-class evangelicals have the power to ignore unpleasant social and environmental realities and ride out the storms until the rapture.

I believe in true apocalypse. I believe in a full uncovering of what is wrong to lead us to new longings, to best practices for rest. Even as we lose and lose and lose. Because in the losing there is nothing hidden. In full, plain light there is hope for restoration, no matter what afflictions we have before us. There is no escape from human suffering in the end. But God's Spirit is a revelator resting near the broken in body, heart, and mind.

CHAPTER 4

One Way

Hippies are hazy, mythic creatures of the mind. Maybe your mom or grandma talked about being a hippie. Maybe there is still sprouted bread instead of Wonder Bread in her kitchen. Or oversaturated photos in her album in golden hour '60s light. There she is, wearing beads and paisley.

The hippie movement, the primary counterculture movement of the '60s, felt old-timey but still compelling to me when I was growing up. When I talk about counterculture, I'm referring to movements within society that critique and push back against elements of normative culture. Countercultural movements tend to attract the youth of a generation and create a shared aesthetic propelled by fashion, art, and music: beats of the '50s, hippies of the '60s, punks of the '70s, goths of the '80s, and grunge kids of the '90s, when I was in high school. Counterculture usually assimilates over time and becomes mainstream. Case in point: flannels were for sale on the racks in my Indiana Target by my sophomore year.

Counterculture critiques dominant narratives. With a healthy dose of rebellion, some teens are drawn to counterculture when differentiating their identity. From a Christian lens, I've always valued the richness and value in counterculture when it brings a prophetic voice to the church and a fresh aesthetic.

Joan Didion's seminal essay on '60s counterculture, "Slouching Towards Bethlehem," ran in the *Saturday Evening Post* in 1967, the same year as the Summer of Love. You don't have to read Didion's piece for more than a few pages to realize that hippies came of age in an era with a lot of pain—and many young people spent a season of choosing a posture to hug the pain, sleep with it, and numb it completely with every possible hallucinogenic and narcotic.

Didion writes about a man named Norris, one of the many hippies she spent time with in Haight-Ashbury while researching for the essay. "One day Norris asks how old I am," she writes. "I tell him I am thirty-two. It takes a few minutes, but Norris rises to it. 'Don't worry,' he says at last. 'There's old hippies too.'"[1]

Beyond drugs and sex, there was a lot of longing, some wandering, for young people in the Vietnam era. Reading Didion's essay, I noticed how everyone seemed to have one foot out the door. *Maybe I'll go to Big Sur. Maybe I'll make my way to New York City.* The feeling, in general, from a lot of hippie accounts of the era: *I've got to get to the next destination.*

Maybe that's one reason why the Jesus Movement was revolutionary. Images of hippie Christians listening to folk music in coffeehouses and living in intentional communities did not just document a transformation of the heart but the creation of a home for the weary. The Holy Spirit was a settler, moving Jesus People from spiritual wandering to rest.

Coastal Conversions

Photos and video from mass baptisms during the Jesus Movement document converts perched on the coastal rocky crags. Hippie preacher Lonnie Frisbee and pastor Chuck Smith, founder of the megachurch Calvary Chapel, baptized thousands of Jesus People underneath the cliffs of Corona del Mar. Frisbee looked like the lead in *Jesus Christ Superstar,* dunking robed bodies in the decades before he died at age forty-three from complications related to AIDS.

Smith recalled the first time Jesus People attended a Sunday church service.

> I heard bells tinkling. Then here came 15 kids, most of them with these tiny strings of bells tied around their ankles. And they did have flowers in their hair. You could almost hear an audible gasp from the rest of the congregation.[2]

Dad was a preppy, nervous Jewish kid from the Midwest who had little interest in hippie counterculture. But as a convert to Christianity who came to faith in the same era as the Jesus People, Dad held the same premillennial view of a coming rapture. His hippie Christian peers also studied *The Late Great Planet Earth.*

Like the early church, Jesus People believed that Christ would return in their lifetimes. Most were premillennial dispensationalists, reading the same literal interpretation of the book of Revelation I was taught by Dad as a kid. It fueled their street evangelism and ministries. As Larry Eskridge writes in *God's Forever Family*:

> In almost every instance where an evangelical pastor, evangelist, or youth worker helped establish or supported a Jesus People group, they brought dispensational teachings with them . . . whether in Bible studies, sermons, informal raps, or tapes and literature, straight evangelical collaborators and enablers of the Jesus movement, like Chuck Smith at Calvary Chapel, regularly turned to the prophetic to snare audience interest. In the process, they presented them with the full gamut of dispensational teachings, such as the importance of Israel, the secret Rapture of the church, the appearance of the Antichrist, and the horrors of the Tribulation.[3]

Late Great connected a "literal" read on the book of Revelation with current events and hit at the right time, when Dad and millions of others in his generation were eager to find an underlying condition that could explain the cultural and social unrest in their midst.

End-times culture also offered a sense of escapism that was rooted in celebration. A buzz of possibility was in the air. For example, a college friend's parents were members of the folk band Armageddon Experience who performed their hopeful, earnest song "One Way!" during Explo '72. This evangelical gathering sponsored by Campus Crusade for Christ filled the Cotton Bowl in Dallas with a reported eighty thousand Jesus People, youth group kids, and college students from across the country. Armageddon Experience sounds like a death metal band destined for a "Parental Advisory: Explicit Language" sticker. Instead, it was composed of hippie kids who could be mistaken for members of The Monkees joyfully singing, "Have you considered Jesus? . . . Has anyone told you he loves you?" while a sea of almost all white faces sang along and swayed.[4]

The Nostalgia Pendulum

Pop culture and fashion tend to come around again in thirty-year cycles, a phenomenon called the "nostalgia pendulum."[5] Fast-forward from the '60s to '90s; hippies had both feet planted in middle-age by the time I started high school. In those years, '60s- and '70s-era maxi dresses, poly button-downs, chunky jewelry, and tchotchkes stashed in basements and attics were being sorted and donated with abandon. My friends and I thrifted as many of these pieces as we could, mixing up geometric dresses and poly button-ups with styles from skateboarding, hip-hop, and grunge.

Taking a nod from the '60s-era Christian folk coffeehouses that popped up as alcohol-free alternatives in college towns across America, in the '90s, churches rediscovered the weekend coffeehouse trend. In my Indiana hometown, and later in the small town near my university, my friends and I would drive to various churches on Friday nights. We'd drink very sweet caramel lattes, listen to bands, and sheepishly read poems on stage.

I attended Cornerstone, a music festival with roots in the '60s every summer around the fourth of July, driving four hours to Bushnell, Illinois. The event tended to gather a merry band of arty Christians that made my own fashion choices—some variation of Dr. Martens boots, plaid pants, a Smiths T-shirt, and a vintage cardigan—look tame. I'd never found more than a few friends with a college rock aesthetic and faith that looked much like my own in my Indiana hometown, and that summertime gathering of cool Christians was a highlight of my year.

The former hippie pastor of my college church in Indiana also worked in coffee. Our church owned a roasting business and ran the coffee tent at Cornerstone each summer, where about twenty of us took shifts selling frozen granitas and Italian sodas. At night, we'd stay up late listening to live music from bands like Luxury, Adam Again, and Ballydowse, a Celtic punk band of Christian activists.

A resident of Bushnell, the tiny farming community where the festival was located, was interviewed for a 2003 documentary commemorating Cornerstone's twenty-year anniversary. "There were an awful lot of people who came to the festival that had unusual hairdos, they had unusual clothes," a city council member said in an interview. The owner of the town's hardware store remembered, "It really surprised me . . . some of the costumes that some of the people wore, and the hairdos. . . . [One] had a big cone shaped about three feet above his head, to a point."[6]

Cornerstone Festival was started in the '80s by Jesus People USA (JPUSA) at a campground an hour outside of Chicago before the event moved a few hours south to Bushnell in the early '90s. The grounds were either dusty or a total swamp if it rained. We'd wash our hair in the lake, go to the medical trailer for Band-Aids, and buy freezer pops at the food tent. There was an art and speaker area offering weeklong "Cornerstone University" programming where musicians, writers, and professors gave talks. I loved these sessions, sitting cross-legged with a journal at the ready during talks about postmodernism and songwriting.

Cornerstone's roster had swelled to a couple of hundred bands by the early aughts. Musician Charlie Peacock summed up the Cornerstone experience in the documentary as, "freethinking people in love with Jesus and in love with music."[7]

In 2011, Cornerstone featured a "Jesus Rally" with bands that had played since the early years of the festival, including Phil Keaggy and Glenn Kaiser's Resurrection Band. Kaiser was an early member and pastor of JPUSA. When an older generation reflects on a movement that defined their youth—when something good peaks and its most potent iteration is in the rearview—there's a certain sadness in the nostalgia.

"All of us are getting older . . . the answer to the critics of the culture is a . . . serious commitment to Jesus Christ," Kaiser said in the 2003 film. "It is not sloppy agape as we used to say in the Jesus Movement Days. It's the real deal. It's the long haul." Kaiser adds, "Stick a mic in our face and say 'What is the Jesus Movement?' and we would literally say, 'Jesus moving' . . . and he still is, he still does."[8]

Eventually, the Ma!l

Hippies wanted to establish an alternative to American culture solidified after World War II. Tie-dye, bell-bottoms, center-parted hair, and folk music are earmarks of hippie style that continue to pop up in the mall every decade. But the aesthetic photographed around San Francisco's Haight-Ashbury neighborhood during the Summer of Love in 1967 was bold and headline-grabbing, because it was fresh.

Hippies were generally against war and big government and for psychedelics and sleeping around. The life of the nomadic, long-haired Jesus of Nazareth looked a lot like hippie life, sans the drugs and sex.

"The Jesus of the Summer of Love was a radical revolutionary who had come to serve the poor, bring about racial harmony, oppose war and violence, and challenge the political establishment," historian Neil J. Young writes in *Vox*. "Beyond embodying the hippies' idealism and radical social vision, Jesus healed the broken dreams and wrecked lives that many hippies felt were the Summer of Love's unexpected consequence."[9] Young continues,

> Months of drug experimentation, free love, and life on the streets began to take its toll on many who had made pilgrimages to San Francisco. For those coming down from a bad trip or reeling from an experience of personal assault —sexual violence was common in the hippie communes—Jesus offered himself as companion and comfort, standing in stark contrast to the judgmental God one often found in churches at the time.[10]

While centered in Southern California, hippie Christians scattered across the country and across the pond. Jesus People established coffeehouses and communes in cities and towns, attracting converts like my college pastor. Hippie Christian counterculture flourished until it became ubiquitous.

By the time I started college, I thought I had found an expression of Christianity that was refreshingly different from the one I learned from my traditional evangelical church back home. My college-era pastor had an open-handed way of expressing thoughts and ideas about the Holy Spirit that could not have been more different from the three-point sermons of the traditional suit-and-tie pastor of my childhood. Additionally, my college pastor welcomed spiritual gifts and valued intentional community and counterculture. Art and expression were encouraged.

It wasn't until much later in life that I realized the two pastors were much more alike than apart in their theology. Both shared a common belief about the end times and coming rapture.

And I learned that as much as hippie Christians started off with an energetic reimagining of how the church could be, many assimilated into an indistinguishable evangelical culture. Some churches that welcomed hippie congregants tacked on "contemporary" services to welcome less suit-and-tie and more jeans-and-T-shirt attendees.

Jesus People–era folk musicians, including Larry Norman, paved the way for CCM.

Norman was interviewed at Cornerstone in 2000, eight years before he died of heart failure. He said this about bands playing that year's festival:

> I feel very sad for Christian music that is not more effective.... The musicianship is great ... but until we really become followers of Christ, pick up the cross, and go through our life into the highways and byways preaching the gospel we're only going to be a subculture. We're not going to be effective.[11]

He was calling out the commercialization of Christian rock: good light shows don't necessarily lead to genuine connection to Jesus or form a distinct counterculture. Christian musicians also weren't talking about hell in the year 2000, and certainly not the rapture. Almost thirty years earlier, Norman had released the song "I Wish We'd All Been Ready," which sounds like a love ballad. I imagine myself in a stadium in 1972, holding up a lighter and swaying as Norman tenderly sings lyrics about a wife who wakes up to find her husband was raptured while she was left behind.

Tarnation

Any Christian movement can be energizing and bring reform, but it can also go off the rails. The structure of the church exists to bring accountability as a counterpoint to the idealism and fervor of movements—but at the same time the institution can become resistant to reform and to God's Spirit.

The legacy of hippie counterculture is tarnished. Some hippie-era communes turned into cults, which made evangelicals like my parents skeptical about anything contemplative or overtly spiritual in the church that could be labeled as an experimental or unorthodox spiritual practice. Cornerstone ended in the aughts, and in 2014 several sexual abuse allegations were levied against members of JPUSA.[12]

The last year I attended Cornerstone, there were too many hands and not enough to do when we were packing up, so I walked around the already empty grounds. A few members from JPUSA were driving golf carts around the property and beginning to break down tents and clean up. Someone left an old couch by the trash bins. I found a discarded end table in good enough shape to keep and put it in my trunk.

Wandering toward the arts and crafts tent, I saw bits of paper confetti and glitter in the grass. I picked up a red ribbon and put it in my pocket with the particular feeling that as much was behind as ahead. The festival was already a ghost, the kind of thing you know will one day be a memory while it's still happening, then too quickly flames out.

Jews for Jesus and Me

Unlike the hippie parents of some of my friends, who grew up listening to Larry Norman and told stories of taking road trips to California to visit Calvary Chapel, neither of my parents were interested in music or hung around coffeehouses or festivals. Dad was quick and nervous enough by nature that he didn't like the idea of drugs making him out of control, which made stereotypical hippie gatherings especially unappealing.

Dad did find a commonality with Christian hippies in both their devotion to *Late Great*–era dispensationalism and their fever for evangelism. He was a lonely Jewish kid who converted to Christianity and was looking for more solidarity. So he was surprised, and energized, to learn about a group of Jewish Christians working at a hippie-focused ministry in Haight-Asbury.

"I thought I was the only Jew in the world who believed in Jesus," Dad says about his conversion. "I had no idea any Jew besides me believed Jesus was the Messiah. Then I found out about Jews for Jesus."

The parachurch organization was founded by Jewish hippies who converted to Christianity in 1970 in San Francisco, three years after the Summer of Love. The ministry officially adopted the name Jews for Jesus in 1973 and expanded its street ministry to gentiles, right around the time Dad got saved. The organization, founded by Moishe Rosen, has grown in the decades since and remains active in cities around the world.

"Capitalizing on the group's growing visibility, Rosen positioned it as a vibrant new outreach to the Jewish people," Eskridge writes, "a particularly vital concern at the time within the evangelical church, given its enthusiasm for dispensational prophetic schemes that books like Hal Lindsey's *The Late Great Planet Earth* had stirred up."[13]

Campaigns on city streets quickly caught the attention of the Jewish community and have been a point of contention ever since. Look up Jews for Jesus on Wikipedia and you'll find the following sentence in the first paragraph: "The group is known for its proselytism to Jews."[14]

A 2006 *New York Times* article that was published ahead of a large planned summer street campaign captures the intensity of emotion from members of the Jewish community toward Jews for Jesus.

> Jewish groups in the city across the religious spectrum, many barely able to contain their loathing for the organization, have united in opposition. Indeed, the response that many people, Jewish or gentile, have to Jews for Jesus epitomizes the derision, admiration and bewilderment that religious proselytizers can engender in this city. To some, they are sterling examples of spirit-inspired boldness; to others, simply infuriating.[15]

Dad fell in the "Spirit-inspired boldness" camp and began to volunteer for Jews for Jesus, eventually leading their "Christ in the Passover" presentation at local churches. When I was twenty, I spent my first summer away from home as an intern at the Jews for Jesus headquarters in San Francisco.

I don't remember much of why I applied for the internship, except that Dad encouraged it and I was interested in journalism and could work on their magazine and live for a few months in a new city. Interns stayed in a Victorian house a couple blocks from headquarters and down the hill from Haight-Ashbury, which by that time was a prime stop for tour buses. I was cautioned by a staff member against going out alone at night but managed to spend evenings and weekends roaming the city, writing poems in an oversized journal.

I spent eight hours a day, Monday through Friday, either working in the office or standing on the street wearing an oversized, red Jews for Jesus T-shirt. The O in "for" was swapped with a Star of David. I joined groups of staff handing out tracts, pocket-sized explainers about salvation. Everyone was positive, congenial, and easygoing. Our own counterculture.

Street witnessing was new and awkward, and it drained me. I remember waiting for someone to spit on me like the stories that were passed between volunteers, but it never happened. Instead, I was usually ignored or approached by street kids or confused tourists asking for directions. I memorized the script and got by.

By the end of the summer, street witnessing was sort of normal. Witnessing in Fisherman's Wharf. Witnessing on Market Street near the Carl's Jr. Witnessing outside the stadium at a San Francisco Giants game. I handed out thousands of tracts. I was every shy kid wearing a sandwich board on your city street corner. I was every kid in a starchy suit knocking, ringing your doorbell, and asking what happens when you die.

Mom and Dad visited me in San Francisco that summer, and the organization's founder, Moishe Rosen, and his wife hosted us for dinner at their home. Dad was so nervous he barely touched his Stouffer's lasagna, his mouth gaping open like he'd just met Moses himself.

After Rosen died in 2010, a *Guardian* article declared, "the death of an extraordinary hate-figure has just occurred."[16] Rosen talked about being the recipient of death threats. He had a knack for leveraging the heated feelings toward him and the organization into support from a broad cross-section of evangelical donors.

A Little Punch

A Barna study from 2019 reported that 47 percent of Millennial Christians think it is wrong to evangelize.[17] I have evangelized. I was just a kid, and trying to tell people about Jesus that summer was ineffective. It was an approach from a different time that traced back to when Jews for Jesus began, in years when the social and cultural climate may have made room for street evangelism in a way that seemed to pack little punch by the '90s. For a few months, I stood in a decades-long line of Jewish Christians passing out little pieces of paper. I wondered how many of the people who took the paper read it. I wondered how many initiated conversations led to further consideration.

The truth is, some probably did. The Jews for Jesus mission statement, "Because faith in Jesus is a viable and thriving expression of Jewish life," holds true. Like many things we try when young, we might regret the experience. We learn from it and wish the people we encountered along the way the best.

Being a half-Jewish person in a small Indiana city with a large white population of residents—most of my peers had hodgepodge German-English-Irish roots—was something I could leverage when I wanted to. Really, it was currency: with my fair skin I could blend in, unlike my Black and Hispanic classmates. I had full access and advantages. Yet I could also leverage my Jewishness as a differentiator if I felt the need to be noticed or embrace the weird power that can come when you're a curious exception. Alongside my love of college rock and vintage clothes, my father was Jewish.

And yet, like my dad's preoccupation with the end times, my Jewishness somehow defined me. I had no control over the defining lines—I was born into them. In me, there is oppressed and oppressor. Majority and minority. I could have been killed for my Jewishness if I was born fifty years earlier, and now I could be the star of the show for a certain generation of evangelicals.

But also in me: my Christianity. "Jesus was a Jew" was a line I heard repeatedly from my parents' church friends when talking about why they love Israel. They were fond of Holy Land tours, modified Passover suppers in church fellowship halls, and Messianic congregations, which were Shabbat gatherings typically made up of a few Jewish Christians but mostly evangelicals interested in Jewish traditions.

Sunday Lunch

Shunned by the local Jewish community after his conversion, Dad found a warm welcome in evangelical circles. When I was a kid, my family would go out for Chinese food after church most Sundays. This meal became a bit of a comedy routine for Dad as he became popular in our nondenominational congregation. "Jews love Chinese food," he'd say to a group of newcomers during coffee hour after the church service. He'd invite them to the Mandarin Inn to keep the conversation going, turning the lazy Susan their way for extra helpings of beef and broccoli and talking about how he met Mom in the Ohio bar, prophecy, and Israel.

The intense interest in Israel from my parents' church friends struck me as odd even as a teen. I'd later learn that their pro-Israel stances were rooted in the dispensationalist eschatology popularized and politicized by the Religious Right in the '70s and '80s and believed by many Jesus People.

Whether they had been hippie or preppy as young adults, the same premillennial, dispensational message made sense to my parents and their friends, who had come up during a tumultuous couple of decades. The world was going to hell, and with end-times prophecy, they had found an escape hatch. The temple? It would be rebuilt in Israel. The Antichrist? He was real and living today. If they were for any reason not raptured, they would not take the mark of the beast on their hand or forehead. They would be beheaded first.

Like pop culture, churches follow generational trends that are easier to assign to specific waves of evangelism after the fact. Seeker-sensitive megachurches tended to attract Boomers. When their

Gen X kids grew up, some stayed in the same congregations. Others left church altogether. Some started house churches or went to Sunday night services at a pub during the Emergent and Missional church eras.

In the early 2000s, more white evangelical churches began moving back, or further into, liturgy and contemplative Christian practices, making room for lament. A growing number of congregations embraced the justice tradition. Church trends blur generational lines, but in general a house church is less likely to attract as many retirees as young professionals, and Millennials are unlikely to attend a traditional Methodist service at a church of mostly older congregants in the city.

The church cycles through the same ideas and approaches to talking about Jesus, attracting people to church, and spreading the gospel. It's been thirty years since church coffeehouses were a thing. Maybe someone will try it again soon, and maybe it will catch on. Or someone will start a new iteration of music festivals that can embrace a vision for Christian counterculture that attracts instead of repels.

But the ubiquity of our online lives, and our exceptional ability to sense when we're being marketed to, should give evangelical growth strategists caution. A better way to expand the church is to first let the call of Jesus overwhelm and change us individually, modeling honest transformation in our own lives.

Counterculture contrasts the dominant narrative. In health, countercultural Christianity isn't an expression of the church resisting any threats to religious liberty or freedom of religion. Instead, a healthy Christian counterculture uses creativity and imagination to press against dominant culture, centering others' stories like Jesus did—never to estrange us but to move us toward greater belonging.

PART TWO
CULTURE WARS

CHAPTER 5

Old Fear, New Age

Sometimes, salvation splinters. When growing up in a non-denominational evangelical church, I picked up on the assumption that certain people were in the kingdom. Others were "only God knows," but . . . probably out. The status of my own personal salvation was a sprouted seed of uncertainty that grew along with me.

I intuited ideas about other denominations and Christian traditions as a kid that I needed to unlearn as a young adult. For example, Pentecostals may be technically under the evangelical tent, but their churches were to be avoided. They were emotion chasers and Holy Ghost addicts. Their churches missed Jesus because they were looking for some conjured magic. Or the Quakers were the same as Mennonites, either overly political or too wholesome and formal. The concept of a Quaker clearness committee wasn't introduced to me until a grad school class on spiritual discernment. Reading Quaker theologian Richard Foster for the first time in my twenties was revelatory.

Catholicism was under suspicion too, perhaps even dangerous. Roman Catholics who believed in transubstantiation—that during communion they drank the actual blood and ate the physical flesh of Christ—were not interested in what my family called a "literal" interpretation of the Bible. Ironically, transubstantiation is based on what many considered a literal interpretation of Scripture resulting from a debate in France in the 800s. It wasn't until my midthirties that I started to explore spiritual direction and the examen. These Ignatian practices had a heavy hand in leading me out of a decade-long spiritual desert.

Dark Crystals

While avoiding the hyperspirituality of Pentecostalism and the hyper-formality of Catholicism, plenty of run-of-the-mill evangelicals in the '80s were aware of the dangers of crystals and how meditation could open the unguarded heart to evil spirits. Some evangelicals braced in a defensive posture when it came to the spiritual world, ready to combat any manifestations of demons and Satan. We were ready for the "bad side," but we did not seek to benefit from the "good side" by making room for the possibility of witnessing the Holy Spirit's work in the world.

Like an enemy circling in the woods, the idea of evil manifestations waiting to pounce especially frightened me as a child. I believed I had the power to let them in. I wondered, Could I take action, even commit a sin by accident, that would somehow open myself up to the devil? Questions of the authenticity of my salvation were constant.

Evangelicals like my family took verses like Matthew 12:31, "And so I tell you, every kind of sin and slander can be forgiven, but blasphemy against the Spirit will not be forgiven" very literally. I cultivated a tangible and consistent fear of committing an unforgivable sin, worried I might execute a single, momentary wrong that would dictate my eternal state of affairs. If my heart was not guarded, my soul would not be recoverable. Thoughts of separation from God poured salt on the wound: Jesus would come back before I would be able to right grave wrongs.

The 1973 film about the demonic possession of a girl, *The Exorcist*, paralyzed me with fear for the entirety of seventh grade. When

I watched the movie, the possessed girl was my same age. The dark, thickly quiet mood of the film stayed on me like an extra blanket when I tried to fall asleep each night.

If you saw this movie as an adult, it might be unsettling. But as a young Christian kid with a dad wary of tarot, games like "light as a feather, stiff as a board," or any other activity that could welcome demons to an otherwise innocuous sleepover, it was resonant. In the film, the girl becomes possessed after playing with a Ouija board. She did something to spark her body being overtaken. I can feel a thread of old fear in my stomach even now, as I write these words three decades later. My scalp is tingling like it does when I watch a horror film.

The Exorcist messaged to me that the enemy of my soul was not only real and vicious but I was also involved—my agency, choices, and thoughts could, willingly or innocently, lead to complete loss of control. And that possibility, that I could think or do something to push God away or be overcome by evil, was all-consuming for years to come.

Theology that hypes up precarity tells us that at any moment we could irrevocably ruin our souls for eternity. It leverages fear as a salvation tactic instead of grace. But salvation is a gift from God. It is not fleeting, like a passing obsession or rumination. Our faithfulness or waywardness do not change the nature of God.

Along with many of my evangelical peers, I grew up with parents and church leaders who have, unwittingly or tacitly, followed a fear-based salvation template that bypassed spiritual formation. Those of us raised in families who were suspicious of Christian spirituality and contemplative practices may have inherited an impoverished version of faith.

Without clear spiritual formation, Gen X and Millennial kids also weren't set up to thrive as we entered adulthood and left the cloister of youth groups or campus ministries. And as my peers and I were starting out in the world, the American church was becoming increasingly politicized and further steeped in culture wars.

Parents of my Christian friends remembered when The Beatles learned about transcendental meditation from the Indian guru Maharaji Mahesh Yogi in the late '60s. Also, the Moonies were gaining popularity, reincarnation became a topic du jour, and world religions began to flavor the West. With the rise of these competing ideologies, Jesus People, who had awakened to their faith in a time of unbounded, radical spirituality, now needed to plant a firm stake in the ground to "engage rival truth claims and maintain boundaries against theological error."[1]

While there are faithful Christians living in theologically orthodox communes today, mostly referred to as "intentional communities," their legacy is complex. The majority of communes, Christian or otherwise, didn't last. Still, there is appetite for communal living today; plans often feature individual homes built on shared land with a central gathering space. According to a 2019 *New Republic* article, the numbers of "ecovillages, co-housing settlements, residential land trusts, communes, and housing cooperatives listed in the Foundation for Intentional Community's global directory nearly doubled between 2010 and 2016, from 679 to about 1,200."[2]

As the years went on, some hippie-era utopian communes that attracted Jesus People turned into cults. For example, Children of God members documented tragic accounts of abuse from pedophilic members, led by a founder who claimed "God was love and love was sex."[3] The group was renamed "The Family" in the late '70s.[4] Another commune that grew in the '60s and '70s, The Way International, rejected an orthodox view of the Trinity.[5] A friend who grew up on a Way campus remembers signs posted around the property that read "SIT," a reminder to Speak in Tongues.

By the time most hippies were middle-aged, their golden years were shown back to them in pop culture that was tinged either with nostalgia or "far out" druggie tropes. My friends' parents who were hippies rarely mentioned it. If the topic did come up, it surfaced either as teen annoyance, "Mom makes us eat healthy food like she used to in the '60s. Everything is sprouted," or deep-blushed embarrassment. In my hometown, the local health food shop was still humming along in the '90s, tubs of tahini and condiments sold by staff wearing socks with sandals and hemp chokers from another era.

Dangerous Rainbows

The term "New Age" generally raises a range of bright red flags for older evangelicals. For Dad, New Age included everything from doing yoga to buying crystals to practicing transcendental meditation. *The Hidden Dangers of the Rainbow: The New Age Movement and Our Coming Age of Barbarism* was written in 1983 by another Fort Wayne native, Constance Cumbey. It was one of the first publications to critique the New Age movement from an evangelical perspective. The book was linked to conspiracy theories and mostly discredited after it was published, but Cumbey did help surface the idea that the New Age movement had enmeshed itself within churches and infiltrated everything from the idea of zero population growth to Montessori education. Not to mention health food stores, which Cumbey claimed were fronts for "New Age recruiting centers."[6]

The actress Shirley MacLaine was in the evangelicals' hot seat in the '80s. MacLaine, then in her fifties, made headlines as a proponent of New Age consciousness. A 1987 *Los Angeles Times* article highlights MacLaine's $300, two-day New Age workshops. Their goal was to help attendees lessen stress and tap into an "unlimited soul."

MacLaine tells the reporter that "The New Age movement is comprised of mostly successful people," and that

> churches are saying you will find God through poverty, but they want to enjoy material success. Religion wants their allegiance, their power. But successful people don't like to give away their power, they like to use their own power to be successful. So there's a contradiction

with a spiritually expanding person, who is also successful, remaining with the church.[7]

Dad would never admit it, but MacLaine was onto something. At least in my family. We didn't remain in church while wishing we could escape, because church was familiar, safe, and a social circle. But we also prized upward mobility, and to the untrained eye it would appear we were more successful at being middle-class, white Midwesterners than Christians. We didn't get there from a new state of consciousness but rather from a fervor for consumerism. With a suspicious posture toward the spiritual, my family's experience of evangelicalism offered little inoculation against materialism and American consumerist culture. The market was quick to swoop further into the white evangelical church as the '80s and '90s unfolded. As we'll explore more in the next section, consumerism was our Christian formation.

Family Ties

My family loved Jesus, and my parents tried to center our family around the Christian story. We dropped a check in the offering plate on Sunday. We purchased Christian-themed trinkets including promise rings, WWJD bracelets, and inspirational placards at the Christian bookstore.

I read in Scripture that we were supposed to be set apart, a new creation in Christ. But in trying to look like everyone else at church, we ended up buying like everyone else, too, to support Christian industry. We also spent energy that would have been better directed toward the deep resources that have connected and sustained the church throughout time.

White evangelical churches assimilated to suburbia, where they had room to grow in modeling how to be "in but not of" the world. So a lot of my peers and I left home for the city when we launched out on our own. We grew up in a suburbia devoid of different perspectives, and we wanted to move away as soon as possible to avoid buying a place on the same block as our parents. New York and San Francisco, where I spent summers in undergrad, symbolized escape. In *Generation X*, the seminal book dramatizing the ethos of people born in the mid-60s through 1980, Douglas Copeland writes, "When someone tells you they've just bought a house, they might as well tell you they no longer have a personality. . . . It's profoundly depressing."[8]

While some strict families limited what their family watched on TV, most of my evangelical friends watched the same commercials between sitcoms that the rest of the country saw. My family watched the Christian Broadcasting Network with sixty million other viewers,[9] but only if nothing better was on the networks.

For many, the counterculture of our parents' generation gave way to middle-class living. Along the way, aging hippies tended to remain comfortable mixing politics and religious practice.

As members of my parents' generation moved from hippies to yuppies, we watched Donald Trump slip into the persona of a "successful" professional person on screen. We first saw Trump emerge as a business guru on *Lifestyles of the Rich and Famous*, and years later we were entertained by his weekly "you're fired" trope on *The Apprentice*. That's where we met the persona of a commander-in-chief who would give evangelicals the deal they wanted in the Supreme Court. It didn't matter if Trump was a bad boss or a gross boss—as long as his company paid out returns.

Conservative Counterculture

Many Christian kids like me saw Trump on television, but not all of us. A 2000 *New York Times* magazine piece considered the rise of conservative evangelical subculture that followed President Clinton's impeachment trial, when the Religious Right experienced a temporary power paralysis that turned some toward a posture of withdrawing from the world.

The feature followed the Scheibner family, fundamentalist Baptists raising their children off the pop culture grid. "The way they practice their faith puts them so sharply and purposefully at odds with the larger culture that it is hard not to see the Scheibners," essayist Margaret Talbot writes, "conservative and law-abiding though they are, as rebels."[10]

The Scheibners are profiled as an example of conservative Christian counterculture. Talbot notes that the family's values, including a vigilant avoidance of pop culture, lack of engagement with public education, and focus on thrift and courtship, "buck mainstream notions of what constitutes a fulfilled life" and embody radical values that are distinct from but follow the same pattern of counterculture.

"That sounds odd to many of us—especially, perhaps, to secular liberals, who cherish our own 60's-inflected notions of what an 'alternative lifestyle' should look like," Talbot writes. She notes that since academic Theodore Roszak initially used the term "counterculture" in the late '60s, it has been associated with "the embryonic base of New Left politics, the effort to discover new types of community, new family patterns, new sexual mores . . . new personal identities on the far side of power politics."[11]

The same year, theologian Miroslav Volf wrote a response to Talbot's article, originally published in *The Christian Century*. "I have tended to think of such people as well-intentioned but naive folk who believe that they can replicate for themselves the world of their pious grandparents. Which is my definition of fundamentalism," Volf writes. "But instead of complaining about the particulars of a robust fundamentalist counterculture, we should ask ourselves: Why are we seemingly incapable of creating a viable and vibrant alternative?"[12]

When bent to the right instead of the left, Christian counterculture can take on a posture of cloistering from a broad secularism. This literal anti- or "away from" culture take on counterculture is a wide correction from hippie Christians. The Scheibners contrast many middle-class evangelicals who adopted a suburban American life light on formation and heavy on sugared cereals. And still others with Jesus People roots moved into a broad spirituality that colored far outside the lines of Christian orthodoxy.

Color, Shape, Sound

What does healthy Christian counterculture look like in our present day? In *The Prophetic Imagination*, Old Testament scholar Walter Brueggemann writes,

> Our culture is competent to implement almost anything and to imagine almost nothing. . . . It is the vocation of the prophet to keep alive the ministry of imagination, to keep on conjuring and proposing future alternatives to the single one the king wants to urge as the only thinkable one.[13]

Imagination can draw us toward a different way of seeing the everyday Christian life. It can spur us to welcome the stranger, because creativity often normalizes ideas that are new and even a little strange.

Historian Mark Noll wrote in the mid-90s that the scandal of the evangelical mind is that there isn't much of one to be found.[14] I'd tack on that the scandal of the Christian aesthetic is that there has become no Christian aesthetic. And without gutsy people writing and making music and art, there can't be a new Christian counterculture.

The church has been so busy fighting culture wars and drawing lines in the sand that we've made little room for broad strokes of imagination. When a church backs away from engagement in the arts and culture, we lose the opportunity to manifest living love in color, shape, and sound.

The Christian life is more vivid with big imagination. In health, Christian counterculture can be a way for those of us who don't quite fit to truly belong—and for us to make welcome Christians with a fresh perspective who have been cast to the margins.

Counterculture is often a natural prophetic voice in society and can form a prophetic function in the church by critiquing the status quo. Counterculture can be leveraged into activism. It can wake people up. For the church, the calling of Jesus brings us out of insular perspectives. There is less to protect when we are more concerned about creating.

Consumerism tells us to live in the city or move away from it or gentrify it. To make art that's weird but commercial enough to sell. To find a microcosm of people like us and preach to the choir. To always want to be famous, or at least social media famous, but to not talk about it. But consumerism is empty, because it is about serving the ego of self, and there is a spiritual vacancy that comes with it.

It's not just Christians that kill counterculture. It's also the way of the market. Commercializing counterculture is not always bad; scaling ideas to reach more people has its own value. It's possible to live an authentic, values-centric life as a Christian supporting and creating art and ideas in a sustainable, and even a holy, posture. But when the smoke machine comes in, when the growth strategy is implemented, the heat of the movement eventually starts to seep out, then evaporate.

A Big Tent of Deep Belonging

Counterculture is not an institution. Church is. The structure of the church exists to bring accountability as a counterpoint to any skewed idealism and fervor of countercultural movements. But at the same time the institution of the church can become resistant to reform and new movements of God's Spirit. And any movement, Christian or otherwise, can be energizing and bring improvement to surrounding systems.

Jesus was not a megachurch pastor or a preacher wearing formal vestments. Be it countering the rigidly religious establishment in

Jerusalem or the Roman Empire, Jesus was both countercultural and drew everyone to belonging. His invitation wasn't an either-or. And like Jesus, his church can again be a big tent with all nations imagining a strangely beautiful and universally compelling future.

CHAPTER 6

Hot Buttons[1]

L ike many kids who grew up evangelical, I was taught that abortion was the only issue when it came to politics. When I turned eighteen, my father took me to the Allen County Republican headquarters in my Indiana town, where I registered as a card-carrying conservative. Then we went to Fort Wayne's Famous Coney Island for celebratory chili dogs.

"It doesn't matter who is president for a term or two," Dad told me. "We vote for the candidates who want to protect the dignity of human life." And those candidates were all in the Republican Party.

Though abortion was the core battle, I have seen evangelicals rally around various flags of the culture wars. One of the first of these I remember was when Andres Serrano's photograph of a crucifix suspended in urine caused a backlash among evangelicals. Dad said it was a disgrace; I agreed with him.

Neither of us knew that Serrano was Catholic—not that this knowledge would have made us more sympathetic to him—or took seriously the interpretation that the piece was a reaction to the exploitation of Christian iconography. To us, and to the church and broader community to which we belonged, it was blasphemy. And it was worth raising hell over.

A lifetime raised in a culture prepared to go to war over any perceived immorality made it especially disorienting to me when Donald Trump rode down a golden escalator into the presidential campaign and captured 81 percent of the white evangelical vote. Trump mocked a reporter with physical disabilities, bragged about groping women, and retweeted comments likening him to "the second coming of God." He was accused by multiple women of sexual assault. He claimed he didn't pray to God for forgiveness.

But instead of triggering outrage in defense of a basic sense of morality, Trump seemed to engender only greater loyalty among white evangelicals. This loyalty remained no matter what the American president said or did, including scattering a peaceful protest with aggressive riot-control tactics after the killing of George Floyd—apparently so he could leave his bunker in the White House, walk to a church, hold a Bible upside down, and have a photo taken.

"We don't like him," evangelical friends told me, "but we don't have a choice if we believe in religious liberty and the sanctity of life." They sounded a lot like my father delivering his Coney Island argument for one-issue voting back in 1996.

The Trump administration offered evangelicals a conservative Supreme Court, and with it, the possibility of *Roe v. Wade* being overturned. But at the heart of the 2020 election, more than abortion, religious liberty, or any other single issue, was fear. White evangelicals were afraid of losing their dominance over people who looked and lived differently from them. They were afraid to lose power, and Trump guaranteed access to it.

But about 19 percent of the millions of white voters who identify as evangelical did not vote for Donald Trump in 2016, and millions did not vote for Trump in 2020. I'm one of them. Evangelicalism has always been a big tent, and I'm in it too.

I related completely with this passage from political commentator David French about the surreal experience of watching evangelical friends and family vote for Trump: "I didn't just watch his political and spiritual takeover of the GOP. I lived it. I experienced friends and family members moving from disgust, to acceptance, to holding their nose and voting, and then to celebrating the man they once reviled."[2]

Yet, even though the church is deeply divided, I've witnessed generative love and kindness from many conservative Christians I may disagree with about significant issues of our day. It's not a simple "us versus them." Jesus is in the work of changing, transforming, and refining all of us. But the polarizing forces in our society are making it harder for us to face differences.

Like millions of other American Christians, I'm politically progressive and I also believe in the sanctity of all life—whether in the womb or out. I attend an Anglican church, but pretending my roots aren't in evangelicalism would be disingenuous.

I know many evangelicals who protested after the death of George Floyd and Breonna Taylor—we are, without hesitation, denouncing racism. Many of us are pro–all of life. We're against the death penalty, denounce white supremacists, welcome refugees, and believe in equal pay for women and equal rights for all people. As a member of the vestry at my church, I've helped provide homeless teenagers with meals purchased from minority-owned restaurants that struggled to stay open during the pandemic. Like those in thousands of other churches, we show up for our cities.

The millions of us who stand against Trump are holding on to hope that the good work Christians do out of the spotlight can salvage our public witness and outshine the hypocrisy burning brightly from our ranks. The work of rebuilding begins with following the lead of our brothers and sisters from various racial and ethnic backgrounds and bringing old sins of racism and sexism into new light. By lifting up just about anyone Trump has belittled to gain dominance.

Christians are called to not just tolerate but also to welcome the stranger and serve the poor. To be hospitable, not judgmental, to people across racial, gender, and socioeconomic lines. To do a better job of listening, repenting, and voting with the marginalized and the underprivileged.

Overwhelming white evangelical support for Trump remains. But regardless of the outcome of the next (or any) election, there is a sizable remnant of evangelicals who persist in choosing human flourishing over fear.

Check the Box

Some days, that remnant feels smaller than others. Especially when I read culture war–infused headlines like "60% of White Evangelicals Believe the 2020 Presidential Election Was Stolen. No Other Religious Group Comes Close"[3] and "The Capitol Riot Revealed the Darkest Nightmares of White Evangelical America: How 150 Years of Apocalyptic Agitation Culminated in an Insurrection."[4]

A culture war, broadly, is the conflict between two groups over specific social beliefs. In the '80s and '90s, American evangelicals found ourselves (or plopped ourselves, depending on our vantage point) in the middle of culture war debates surrounding evolution in schools, the canon of Western literature, sexual identity, and, again, abortion. Anyone raised evangelical during this time, like me, probably belonged to a church that leaned conservative on political and cultural issues, including an opposition to abortion and same-sex marriage.

Many of these topics had been building as tension points since the sexual revolution. In his 2015 book *A War for the Soul of America*, historian Andrew Hartman says that before the '60s, "normative America" was baseline. The majority of the population tended to agree on matters like gender roles and patriotism. While we had the beats, progressive scholars, and outsider artists in the '40s and '50s, counterculture was fairly tempered. It wasn't until the cultural revolution in the '60s—with hippies, anti-war protesters, second-wave feminists, and gay and civil rights advocates populating headlines—that white American Christians began to hear more defined messages of dissent. There were folks straddling both categories in the church and culture, like Jesus People and white civil rights allies, but as a whole, white Christians fell into the "normative" camp.

The culture wars unified evangelicals like Dad in a single-minded pursuit to oppose abortion. Abortion came to define American evangelicalism in the '70s, and the issue continues to play a key role in politics today, especially after Roe's overturn in June 2022. Here is a high-level, unspoken message shared between Christians who are against abortion: "We are the protectors of the unborn. We have clear consciences by proxy because we believe in the welfare of those who cannot protect themselves." There is an undertone of judgment in this posture, an in and out group that paints broad strokes over the conversation.

When we tie up faith with a single issue, the church is impoverished. Doing so boils down the Christian tradition, in its rich global expressions and history, to one focal point, as if Jesus came two thousand years ago simply to transform US laws around reproductive health.

That energy could have gone into the church and worked for flourishing in a myriad of ways. Instead, cynicism and skepticism took root. We heard a lot of talk from leaders about caring for the unborn but saw little follow-through. Many non-Christians were the most vocal in speaking up for human rights and dignity, while some evangelicals simply pulled a lever in the ballot box to vote down the party line and called it a day. The message I heard growing up is that our civic duty as Christians was fulfilled when we voted for pro-life candidates.

Young Single Mother

When I was in high school, I showed up one morning at the local Planned Parenthood clinic in downtown Fort Wayne with about thirty classmates. We stood on the curb and waited for women to enter the clinic for appointments. Whenever a woman was escorted to the door, we hung our heads and prayed. It was emotional and heavy. One classmate, a staunch Democrat who seemed to have ended up in our Lutheran high school by no choice of her own, stood alone across the street holding a pro-choice sign toward our group.

This was the single instance I showed up at the clinic. I knew Christian groups met at Planned Parenthood often to pray or try to hand out leaflets as women entered for appointments. On the other hand, I did not know anyone who worked to support young single mothers. We left that to aid agencies and social services, assuming the state must have some program or another to help get teen moms on their feet. Maybe there was an Indiana government office with a closet full of care packages with diapers, wipes, and a few jars of Gerber baby food.

David Barnhart, a pastor in Alabama, illustrates this idea with potency:

"The unborn" are a convenient group of people to advocate for. They never make demands of you; they are morally uncomplicated, unlike the incarcerated, addicted, or the chronically poor; they don't resent your condescension or complain that you are not politically correct; unlike widows, they don't ask you to question patriarchy; unlike orphans, they don't need money, education, or childcare; unlike aliens, they don't bring all that racial, cultural, and religious baggage that you dislike; they allow you to feel good about yourself without any work at creating or maintaining relationships; and when they are born, you can forget about them, because they cease to be unborn.[5]

My mother, who became pregnant as a teenager in the 1970s and had a baby who was adopted through Catholic Charities, volunteered at a local crisis pregnancy center for a few years. Whenever I see a billboard advertising how early a young heartbeat begins or an ad for a pregnancy resource center like the one where my mom volunteered, I wonder what circumstances these young clients find themselves in before making an appointment. Do they know the person on the other side of the desk will present options for adoption, and that the office is likely run by Christians? At the end of the year, Mom would receive a Christmas card with handwritten names of the babies who were saved from abortion the year before. We put it on the fridge: living proof that there is another way.

We threw it in the trash with other cards when we took down the tree and lights each year. No one thought about what would happen to these names, now that they had experienced their first Christmas. They were alive, and that was what mattered.

The Unborn and the Born-Again

Evangelicals as a whole were largely disengaged with abortion through the '60s and into the mid-70s, although it was a central issue for some Protestants and many anti–birth control Catholics for decades prior.[6]

The Religious Right launched six years after abortion was legalized, when conservative strategist Paul Weyrich leveraged abortion as an evangelical battle cry to elect Republican candidate Ronald Reagan instead of Democratic incumbent (and Southern Baptist) Jimmy Carter in 1980.[7]

President Carter had a memorable style by way of cozy button-up cardigans, but during his four years in the Oval Office he did little to secure the trust of the evangelicals who helped elect him. Carter had been criticized since midway through his presidency for focusing more on process than policy,[8] and is mostly remembered for failing to secure the release of American diplomats and citizens held hostage during the takeover of the American embassy in Iran in 1979.

Evangelicals who had been leaning Republican since the end of World War II were catalyzed by the Cold War—and by evangelist Billy Graham's public support of Eisenhower and Nixon. With Carter floundering, they were ready to welcome a stronger conservative alternative into the Oval Office.

Politics is an exchange, and the Religious Right had an agenda. The strategist Weyrich had been throwing noodles at the wall for years—school prayer, pornography—looking for a key issue that would stick for evangelicals. He was not searching to right a particular wrong but to find a topic that could move voters toward the Republican Party.[9]

The rise in the number of legal abortions after Roe passed in 1973 helped highlight abortion as the issue that would finally ignite evangelicals into a wide, energized base. The freshly mobilized conservative-voting constituency played a large part in Reagan's successful presidential bid and included evangelical leaders like Jerry Falwell of Liberty University, who founded political action group the Moral Majority in 1979.

Yet, as religion historian Randall Balmer explains, the origins of the Religious Right are more complex than the abortion debate and are directly linked to segregation.

At Bob Jones University, there was a ban on interracial dating until 2000,[10] even though the Supreme Court ruled in 1967 that laws preventing interracial marriages were unconstitutional.[11] The institution apologized for its former racially harmful actions, such as banning African American students until the '70s, in a statement in 2008.[12]

Bob Jones, Liberty University, and other private educational institutions were concerned about the IRS working to desegregate universities during Carter's term after the schools were flagged for discriminatory admissions policies. In supporting Reagan, the pro-life Falwell earned a bonus win for Liberty. When Reagan took office, he dropped the government inquiry, and segregation remained unchecked at the colleges.[13]

As historians Gillian Frank and Neil J. Young write in a 2022 *Washington Post* op-ed, conservative Christian opposition to abortion was also built from the ground up. Beyond major players in the evangelical world, it's worth noting the

> "thousands of grass-roots activists, religious leaders and conservative thinkers who spent nearly two decades building the networks and ideas that brought about the religious right." Beyond abortion, evangelicals were engaged in "a web of interconnected issues from the 1960s and '70s, including opposition to the proposed Equal Rights Amendment (ERA) to the U.S. Constitution, school prayer, school

integration, changing attitudes about gender and sexuality and the growing gay rights movement. Those issues were shaped directly and indirectly by racist ideas and attitudes and were part of a broader political realignment that moved White Southern evangelicals and Northern White Catholics from the Democratic Party to the GOP in this period."[14]

A lot of families talked about being color-blind when I was a kid. Race had nothing to do with the culture wars, or so was the unspoken assumption I intuited. In a *Publishers Weekly* interview, Balmer notes that the "abortion myth" of the Religious Right—the idea that abortion was at the heart of the movement when it was really rooted in race—still has staying power because of "some sort of visceral identification evangelicals [have] with the vulnerability of the fetus. They see themselves as being vulnerable and victims in this society."[15]

In actuality, women of color are most likely to receive an abortion. A 2019 CDC report found that only 33 percent of women who have abortions are non-Hispanic white while 38 percent are non-Hispanic Black.[16] Women of color are more likely to navigate a myriad of societal and financial obstacles and experience a range of negative outcomes when access to abortion is restricted.

In a five-year study on the socioeconomic impact of women who are denied abortion access, mental and physical health, education, and financial outcomes worsened for women living at the poverty baseline. Women in the study also experienced a four-fold increase in the likelihood their household income fell below the federal poverty line.[17]

While Balmer does not argue that "all grassroots evangelicals are racist," he calls out a "subconscious racial bias" that informs political stances. "It's also notable that evangelicals were not visible on the march from Selma to Montgomery," Balmer says. "They were not in the vanguard of the Civil Rights struggle. And we have to account for that."[18]

My parents did not know about the strategy behind the politicization of abortion; most Christians today don't. Paul Weyrich was never a household name. My parents voted for Carter in '76, who became the country's first president to use the term "born again."

My mother had an emotional investment in teen pregnancy, and my father listened to Christian radio. They were both moderately engaged in political discourse, read the Sunday paper, and believed that the right person in the Oval Office could help Christians make their voices heard. By the time Reagan delivered the line, "If we ever forget that we're one nation under God, then we will be a nation gone under" at a prayer breakfast in the 1984 Republican National Convention, many evangelicals were all in.[19]

There is little value in painting individuals who made up the Religious Right in broad strokes as good or bad, in or out. If your parents were opposed to schools teaching evolution or sex ed, they were a part of a culture war, whether tacitly or actively. They were probably influenced by the moral majority in the late '70s and '80s, whether they heard talking points in Christian media or from the pulpit.

Their votes for Reagan may have been earnest. They could have been acting under social pressure to vote Republican while privately questioning the still-young marriage between the evangelical church and politics. Or they could have been dissenters, people who spoke against any politicization from the pulpit or saw through the Republican-evangelical allegiance to understand it was a way for evangelicals to be in control—and a way for politicians to get elected.

In health, evangelical parents tend to be a lot like other parents: people who want their children to thrive. Most parents believe they're doing the best they can to protect their children and raise them up with a good set of beliefs and worldview. I like to think I've gained discernment and prudence as my political views have shifted as an adult. Surely, though, I'm handing down my own flavor of politics to my children, and time will tell how sound my own stances are—and probably reveal my blind spots.

Satanic Panic

In the 1980s and '90s, the culture wars found conservative legislators and prominent evangelicals working together to remove government-allocated dollars for the National Endowment for the Arts (NEA) following dust-ups with visual artists including Serrano and Robert Mapplethorpe.

In 1990, a Mapplethorpe exhibit with sexually explicit images displayed at the Contemporary Arts Center in Cincinnati was briefly shuttered by law enforcement, and the museum's director was given an obscenity charge. The exhibit came under fire because Mapplethorpe, like Serrano, had received public funding from NEA grants. Congress then voted for legislation requiring the government-funded arts agency to funnel work through a "decency test."[20]

Regardless of how invested they were in censorship toward artists like Mapplethorpe, many of my friends' parents wanted to protect us kids from hidden messages in music. As mentioned earlier, the culture wars reached "low culture" in 1985 when Tipper Gore and other wives of politicians cofounded the Parents Music Resource Center during the Reagan administration. The committee introduced the black-and-white "Parental Advisory Explicit Content" stickers and infamously presented a "Filthy 15" list of songs with offensive lyrics—a designation that these days may make us think of organic produce.

Songs on the list included Madonna's "Dress You Up" for its sexual content, while Twisted Sister's "We're Not Gonna Take It" earned a slot for lyrics the committee deemed violent. Another category on the list of flagged songs were those with "occult" lyrics from heavy metal bands. This "satanic panic" had prompted the committee's formation—a response to the idea held by some evangelicals that the devil controlled the entertainment industry. Sensing a certain allure, us kids promptly crammed around the TVs of friends who had cable and watched metal videos on MTV.[21]

Tipper Gore's committee was active during the years that "back-masking" on records became a household concern for some Christian families. Listeners posited that subliminal messages could open kids up to evil spiritual forces: Queen's stadium anthem "Another One Bites the Dust" contains hidden language about smoking marijuana; Slayer's "Hell Awaits" includes the backtrack "join us"; and Led Zeppelin's "Stairway to Heaven," when played backwards, reveals the words "my sweet Satan."[22] Of course, looking for backmasking became a favorite sneaky hobby of us kids. I have an early memory of sneaking into the den and trying to play the *Footloose* soundtrack backwards to pick up on secret words when my parents weren't in the room.

The Dignity of Choice

The idea of victim and underdog—that God is fighting for evangelicals because we are ridiculed in society—is a distortion of the truly weak, marginalized, and oppressed.

Abortion is a moral issue, and a consistent, whole life ethic is held by many Christians, including myself. But rallying abortion as a concern to put Christians on defense as protectors of the unborn may resonate for some because we, too, are in search of protection from a culture that presses back.

Beyond the slogans, most of us would agree that the dignity of choice is important. Yet one piece that gets lost in the discussion about abortion is pro-choice as a concept. Certain words come with implications. A Christian will most certainly say, "I am pro-life" and not use the language "I am anti-choice" that has been adopted by some progressive voters to describe people who oppose abortion. On the other hand, a Christian may scoff at the concept of "pro-choice," because the point is the baby, duh, and not a woman's right to make a decision about a life that is not her own, even if she is growing the baby inside her own body.

For some, pro-choice as a concept moves beyond pregnancy and is used as a signifier of autonomy. Pro-choice says that women are free to be paid equally to men and to make their own decisions, including about when to be and stay pregnant. Sex, then, is not about childbirth but about pleasure. Pro-life (or anti-choice, depending on your vantage point) as a movement is patriarchal, where a mostly male legislature and court decide what happens to the bodies of women.

My mother, pregnant at seventeen, was sent away by her parents to a Catholic facility in Columbus to have her baby. Her Italian Catholic parents told friends and family she had moved to Ohio for six months for a job training program. In Columbus, my mother remained in the home throughout her pregnancy with other young women. My mother was drugged during labor. She knew she had a boy because she was asked to sign circumcision paperwork. She was not given the option to keep her child.

It is lamentable that people like my mother have been forced into this scenario, the result of a mix of family dynamics and larger cultural mores. As a bearer of God's image, my mother deserved freedom that promotes human dignity while recognizing our interdependence on each other and creation. Instead, what often animates American discussions is a thin sense of freedom based on a myth of rugged individualism.

Republican talking points include freedom of the market, deregulation, and competition. Democrats talk about abortion and other social issues as matters of choice. Each party shares a common view of freedom—and can use it to politicize our sense of agency. While both sides of the aisle fight bitter battles, at their root they're influenced by a capitalistic idea of consumer choice rather than freedom that leads to thriving.

Beyond abortion, the idea of "my body, my choice" has been leveraged by certain conservative voters as a matter of freedom, including some who sought a religious exemption from the Covid vaccine. But there is a difference between supporting dignity and agency and appropriating politicized language to create a false sense of parity. A subset of Americans don't want policy makers to dictate their decisions, even if it is for a community's larger benefit. It's shameful to equate the decision of a pregnant mother forced to make an impossible choice about a pregnancy to the decision of those who would not put on a mask during the pandemic, even in order to care for the immunocompromised like Dad, only because they found it inconvenient.

An Arc of Dignity

Christian voters can hold a pro–all-of-life posture and vote for candidates of either party who uphold the most policies that result in improvements to the quality of life for every person. Policies to support an ethic of personhood rooted in equity, dignity, and esteem.

God is mysterious, working in all things, turning seeds into babies with their own vibrant souls and spirits. We may have been raised to focus on a politicized take on abortion. But the Christian ethic stretches the arc of dignity across many postures in birth, life, and death.

If life is sacred, all of life is then sacred. There is no imaginary scale weighing the life of an unborn baby to be greater than the life of a living child. An aborted child will never have a chance, we might say. But a living child may not have a childhood. Both the unborn and born child are biological creations. The first has been used as a tool to gain election by Republicans for more than four decades. The second is largely ignored by them when it comes to health care and universal pre-K. It's not that evangelicals have made too much of this issue of the sanctity of life. Rather we've set the bar too low for what pro-life can be.

We are called to be pro-immigrant, pro-migrant, and pro-refugee. We are for the oppressed, for minorities, and for women. We also see biblical precedent for being against. We are against the exploitation of children. Against exiling the bright spirits of people made in God's image, regardless of their sexual identity or gender. We are against mass incarceration and the death penalty. We are against the harm spun from commodifying the body through pornography, of using the image of another real-life person as a sexualized dreamscape for the sad glorification of our bent imaginations.

One problem with identifying as single-issue voters is that when everyone knows our next move, it's easy to be manipulated. To date, tallying American presidents from Carter until the beginning of Biden's term in 2021, the United States has been led by a Democratic president for twenty years and a Republican president for twenty years. No matter which party occupied the Oval Office, controlled Congress, or installed justices on the Supreme Court, abortion remained legal until *Roe* was reversed in 2022.

Abortion has been a defining matter for conservative Christians and Catholics for decades. With *Roe* overturned, time will tell if political engagement intensifies or cools—if interests diversify and where the evangelical gaze will shift.

After news broke that *Roe* was overturned, some evangelical leaders were vocal in their support of making America an easier place for single mothers to have children. Is pressing for the broad policy required to come alongside all mothers just lip service, or can the church find backbone to support women and babies in a posture of authentic Christian activism that is both faithful to Scripture and service?

When the decision to have an abortion is personal, impacting a family member or friend rather than a disembodied concept, it becomes nuanced and complex. Anyone who can keep a safe distance from an issue so that it remains conceptual and not consequential is in a privileged position that does not reflect the reality of many citizens.

"Since Roe, our culture has increasingly come to understand that it's not merely 'our bodies, ourselves.' But also 'our communities, ourselves,'" Karen Swallow Prior writes. "Our bodies live and move among other bodies—whether for good or ill. We are our brother's and our sister's keepers, and it does take a village to become who we are."[23]

A Vote for a Bowl of Soup

Politicians chose to center Republican strategy on abortion for many years because it was personal and emotive. Eventually, abortion as a campaign focus—the decades-long firewall of the conservative voting block—had competition. New threats emerged in the 2010s that had the potential to impact the financial security of US households,[24] including concern from some voters about jobs being filled by immigrants instead of white American citizens.[25]

Evangelicals could have formed a Religious Right as a response to American foreign policy, for example, through a campaign in the first half of the 1980s to help Latin American refugees. We could have banded together around the original Sanctuary Movement following the Iran-Contra in Nicaragua and the violence in El Salvador and Guatemala. We could have adopted a new social gospel of direct service and practical care. But we didn't, because Republicanism met evangelicalism wearing a tux on the dance floor, and could he ever dip and sway.

The church is called to disciple Christians as we make ethical choices in the midst of the marketplace of politics, art, and ideas. The church's job is not to tell us how to vote but to be a prophetic voice holding all political parties to account. Politicians, in return, should be prepared to meet voter concerns on both sides of the aisle.

Our vote, whoever it is for, is valuable and precious. We should not sell it, like Esau selling his birthright for a bowl of soup, to any politician or political party after strategists poll voter blocks to settle on talking points that will capture our attention. Instead, we can prayerfully consider the wide range of issues that can make our democracy, shared society, and world into a better place.

There is no need for American Christians to fear the removal of our religious liberty. Instead, we can promote pluralism that welcomes all creeds. Because in health, the body politic of the American church values diverse aspects of humanity.

The church should be a spiritual refuge and repository for truth and life. When it becomes synonymous with any political party, the church loses its saltiness. We are no longer a light on a hill but an organization used to turn out the vote.

The church is not living into its calling when we leave behind anyone who thinks or lives differently, orphaning believers marginalized in the culture wars. Historic Christian practice has so much more to say about how to live together and care for each other beyond hot button issues, from radical giving to practical service.

Inclusivity does not necessitate unorthodoxy, and counterculture can draw in and not leave out. We can center our vote and life on Jesus, whoever we are. Christians can move forward, reclaiming our voice to speak against the commodification of the church and adopting a consistent and full ethic of life.

CHAPTER 7

Christian Soldiers

The end of a very long autumn dragged its way toward the holidays. I was weary from caregiving for Dad in a pandemic and following presidential campaign coverage on the news. Election night 2020 stretched on without a winner for almost a week after votes were cast. I woke up the Saturday after the election to my phone ringing. "It's over," my friend Amanda said.

Biden defeated Trump. The kids finally got to pull a dangling string to release the deflating balloon drop we'd been ducking under in the living room doorway since election night. It started to sag a little more each day as the outcome of the election remained unknown. At one point, I wondered if we'd need to pop the balloons instead of letting them fall. A lot of pinpricks releasing trapped air.

Headlines about the Trump administration's call for several statewide recounts continued into the 2020 holiday season. These attempts to overturn an election the Trump campaign deemed rigged were unsuccessful but brought with them the surreal feeling that the whole election cycle would never end.

Some evangelical Trump supporters who voiced concern that the vote had been skewed began to protest in towns across the country. One notable example occurred in mid-December, when thousands of people gathered for the "Let the Church Roar" prayer rally in Washington, DC. The event was one of several hosted by a group called Jericho March, which describes itself as a collection of Christians called to "pray together, sing songs, and blow shofars."[1] The name Jericho March is a nod to the city of Jericho in the Old Testament that Joshua and the Hebrews defeated after marching around the city's wall seven times blowing trumpets. In the DC crowd that day, a "Trump shofar" painted like an American flag was widely photographed, a visual marker in a rally of conservative voters calling foul play on election results.

The stated organizational intent of Jericho March may have been to pray and sing, but the tone of the event was defiant. A crowd of majority white participants listened to speakers, including conservative radio host and conspiracy theorist Alex Jones. "God gave us and rose up Donald Trump to stand against the enemy and draw out the enemy," Jones said from the stage. "This is the beginning of the great revival before the Antichrist comes. World government, implantable microchips, Satanism. It's out in the open."[2]

An American war veteran also delivered a message from the podium that evoked violence, foreshadowing the forthcoming Capitol insurrection. "You can be called up as the militia to support and defend the Constitution. . . . If [Trump] does not do it now, while he is commander in chief," the vet tells the crowd, "we're going to have to do it ourselves later in a much more desperate, much more bloody war."[3]

The DC Jericho March rally occurred a couple of weeks before the attack at the Capitol and attempted insurrection on January 6, 2021. A month later, a majority of Republican evangelicals remained convinced that the insurrection wasn't organized by conservatives at all. A February 2021 poll from the Survey Center on American Life reported that 60 percent of white evangelical Republicans believed the insurrection was led by the leftist, anti-fascist group Antifa, compared with 42 percent of nonevangelical Republicans.[4]

After reports that some insurrectionists also attended Jericho March gatherings, the group's organizers denounced the Capitol attack, stating that "the mission and goal of Jericho March is to exercise and pray for our religious freedoms and other freedoms under the First Amendment of the Constitution of the United States."[5]

My family members and friends who voted for Donald Trump, including Dad, would not have attended the Jericho March "Let the Church Roar" prayer rally. They would not have broken into the Capitol during the insurrection. The evangelical Trump voters I personally spoke with during the election sounded a lot like other evangelical Trump voters I read about. Most used a slightly different version of the now-familiar reasons to explain their vote: "My decision to support Trump is not about him as a person. I believe in what he stands for: a conservative court, pro-life, pro-gun, and pro-business."

Beyond who sits on the Supreme Court, ideas about end times and culture wars influenced some Trump-supporting evangelicals. Consider the comment from Alex Jones that we are at "the beginning of the great revival before the Antichrist comes." These conservative evangelicals were quick to vote for Trump—and call for "election integrity" after he was defeated by President Biden—for good reason: they believed Trump would bring America to a place of prominence as a nation and protect religious liberty until the second coming of Jesus.[6]

A Violent Twist

A shirtless Arizona resident wearing red, white, and blue face paint and Viking horns stood in Congress praying during the insurrection. Quite a bit of media from the events on January 6 in the Capitol building included photos and videos of this man named Jacob.

Jacob stood by the desk where Vice President Pence had sat before the Senate was evacuated minutes earlier, just before protestors stormed the Capitol chamber. At one point, Jacob asked other insurrectionists in the room to stop and pray. A *New Yorker* video records the interaction: he pauses to remove his headdress while some in the room remove their red "Make America Great Again" hats; many bow their heads and lift their hands. It was a potent display of Christian nationalism on a global stage.[7]

Jacob claimed to be a practicing shaman, but his prayer sounded a lot like one that might be delivered in a Sunday church service. He thanked God for "allowing the United States of America to be reborn" and for "filling this chamber with patriots that love you and that love Christ."[8] This prayer is a politicized plea for a specific kind of American renewal that would look a lot like the status quo, with a violent twist.

A year after he was arraigned and pleaded not guilty, Jacob apologized for his actions. "Be patient with me and other peaceful people who, like me, are having a very difficult time piecing together all that happened to us, around us, and by us," he said in a statement. "We are good people who care deeply about our country."[9]

Defining Christian Nationalism

Christianity began two thousand years ago in the Middle East. Christian nationalism is a hollow take on historic Christianity. It is a conservative version of the cut-and-paste religiosity preferred by some members of the general Christianized population, and it was on full display during the insurrection. Christian nationalism seeks to protect dominant white culture and maintain the current state of American affairs in the twenty-first century. It is an appropriation of Christian theology, a dangerous ideological framework that props up Western pride—"God and country."

Christian nationalism does not have a single, textbook definition, but there are common themes that come together to define the worldview. It is distinct from patriotism, or a love of country. It is a good thing to pray for your country and work for its health. A patriot is "a person who vigorously supports their country and is prepared to defend it against enemies or detractors."[10] Christians are patriots when we work to lend vigorous support to all fighters of racial injustice. We are called to stand with and work alongside fellow Americans, immigrants, and refugees.

To contrast patriotism, Christian nationalism is a conflation of the interests of the government with the goals of the kingdom of God, falsely centering America in a salvation narrative and the preservation of white dominance.

Some white people talk about how America used to be when they were younger with a glint in the eye: cheaper, simpler, safer. Back porches and sweet tea. White nostalgia can cast a warm light on a past remembered as golden while erasing colonialist roots. But golden for whom? That light does not shine on the inequity and racism we fail to mention in a "Make America Great Again" narrative.

When white American evangelicals were raising families in the decades before now, nationalism was harder to identify. We were American patriots and we were Christians and that worked fine. For a long time, for those of us with the right skin color, it did.

In contrast with patriotism, which centers on love of country, nationalism centers on how a country is defined, on who is in and who is out.[11] Christian nationalism twists together politics, policies, and culture, attempting to "merge Christian and American identities, distorting both the Christian faith and America's constitutional democracy."[12] Christian nationalism melts God and country together like smashed crayons in a cookie tin. A country of many colors becomes gray-purple.

As the mix of "Jesus Saves" signs, Confederate flags, and "Make America Great Again" hats on display at the Capitol insurrection suggest, Christian nationalism in its worst distortion equates Donald John Trump with Jesus Christ. This message has been enforced by politicians, including former energy secretary Rick Perry, who told Fox News in 2019 that Trump was "God's chosen one." Republican Representative Barry Loudermilk said during Trump's first impeachment trial that, "When Jesus was falsely accused of treason, Pontius Pilate gave Jesus the opportunity to face his accusers. During that sham trial, Pontius Pilate afforded more rights to Jesus than the Democrats have afforded this president in this process."[13]

There are many factors that have shaped Christian nationalism and its impact on the American church, including American exceptionalism, the role of Israel, dispensationalism, conspiracy theories, and totalitarianism. That's a lot of -isms, but by putting them together we can better understand past division and consider a path forward. Looking back helps us peel away the layers of the American Christian story to uncover the difference between nationalist idolatry and following Jesus.

American Exceptionalism

To understand Christian nationalism, a good place to begin is with American exceptionalism, the belief that the history, democracy, and values of the United States are linked to a destiny that will lead the world.[14] That America is the beacon, the light under the bowl that is lifted and spreads.

It's not uncommon for US politicians to link a blessing from God with American prosperity, like this 2015 Facebook post from then presidential candidate Ted Cruz: "God's blessing has been on America from the very beginning of this nation and I believe God isn't done with America yet." Cruz includes a call to action to donate to his campaign at the end of the post.[15] If a country is dominant during a certain era, it is a jump to assume that is true because the country is blessed by God. It is an equally false idea that a country in need of development and flourishing is in a state of want because God has condemned it.

Generational dynamics can also be at play in American exceptionalism. Writer Nick Shindo Street highlights the generational divide around the belief that God has granted America a special role to play in the world:

> Older, whiter evangelical Christians in suburbs and small cities tend to believe that American exceptionalism is tied to the country's instrumental role in establishing God's Kingdom in Israel after a period

of apocalyptic upheaval. Younger, more ethnically diverse evangelicals in urban areas see the Kingdom of God in the here-and-now, with Christian and non-Christian communities cooperating to ease suffering and promote social justice, thereby making America more exceptional.[16]

American exceptionalism with an "older, whiter" evangelical accent sends a message: the decline of America in the world is a result of sin. We've displeased God with our liberalism. Since the sexual revolution of the '60s and a general pressing from secular humanism and the "progressive agenda" that omits God from the equation, the nation has a weakened place in the world because God's favor has turned away from us.

This framework is unbiblical. "Biblically speaking, all human beings are blessed by God by virtue of the fact they are created in his image, and fundamentally equal," Catholic writer William Doino Jr. says in a *First Things* essay. "To regard secular America as some kind of Messiah nation, or geo-political golden calf, is sheer idolatry."[17]

Like Israelites in Exile

American exceptionalism has been a part of white Protestant DNA since the 1500s, when Protestants fleeing Catholicism during the Reformation landed in New England. Pilgrims who arrived here after escaping Europe believed they were delivered by God to America. In this view, just like God had a specific destiny for Israel in the Old Testament, God had a specific destiny in mind for white Europeans planting a nation in a new geographical location.

Instead of extracting hope from the story of Israel, letting it serve as a reminder of God's deliverance, these religious exiles appropriated the story. Seeing an echo of the biblical narrative in their own circumstances, they wrote themselves into history as the true people of God entering the promised land of the New World with divine authorization to clear it of "Canaanite" Native Americans.

Maybe Puritans saw themselves reflected in the stories of dis-placed Israelites in the Old Testament, considering themselves to be delivered exiles and America to be a new promised land of milk and honey. This line of reasoning is threaded into nationalism in our present day, positioning white Protestants to stand in a line of our "exceptional" ancestors whom God had set apart. A Christian nation would see God uniquely work through history to bless us, just like Abraham was promised a blessing for the people of Israel.[18]

In American history, both the white Protestant and Black churches have walked through an exodus. However, here is a hermeneutical distinction: The African American church may see parallels of God delivering Jews in the Old Testament as inspiration and encour-agement for their exile from Africa. But they did not appropriate the biblical story of Exodus and write themselves into it to justify American exceptionalism like white Protestants.[19] Instead, they cel-ebrated what God had done in the past with the people of Israel and gained energy and sustenance. They generated a living hope that, as God had acted on behalf of the oppressed people of Israel in the past, he might act again on behalf of Black Americans. They left the metaphor intact instead of making themselves the biblical protagonists and understood something of who God is throughout the ages, a God of courage and deliverance.

The example of God setting the Israelites aside, preserving them, and carrying them across the Jordan to a new land bears a promise for change. There is radiant hope for restoration from slavery and protection by God, but not a conflation of identity that justifies dominance, protected and individualized, like we find in Puritanism.

Christian nationalists are like Pharisees, hoping to restore Amer-ica into God's blessed land. If they work a little harder, that reality, just out of reach, will come to pass. The Pharisees believed that if they lived rightly and kept Sabbath, the Messiah would return. Jesus's disciples plucking wheat to fill their stomachs on the Sabbath was a scandal, because it was a step away from lawful action that would lead to redemption.

If the Pharisees withheld a little bit more, emptied a little bit more, studied a little more, it might be enough to light the flame and bring their king. But by keeping laws that chose order over compassion, by not lifting anything heavier than a feather, the Pharisees lost empathy. Along the way, they crushed the poor who were a threat to their mission, the means—their oppression—justifying the ends—glory—they tried to work into reality.

With the same posture, Christian nationalists are working for an outcome that remains just beyond their grasp. America has turned away from God as a nation, but maybe we can elbow ourselves back into God's favor. Because, as the line of reasoning goes, America can again be exceptional like before. And maybe if the right person is in the White House, the country can nudge closer to restoration. Restoration that keeps white citizens in power, in jobs, and filling city council seats. There is no room for compassion in this vision for America.

Dispensationalism's Role

Like exceptionalism, dispensationalism has political ramifications. A 2015 poll from YouGov reports that 28 percent of Americans said nuclear war will end the world. Climate change and "judgment day" tied for second place at 16 percent.[20]

But here is a paradox. On one hand, the premillennial dispensationalist view of the book of Revelation sparks little motivation for Christian engagement in environmentalism if the world is headed toward destruction. On the other hand, politically engaged dispensationalists see reason to secure and keep power, driven by paranoia that the world is moving in an ungodly direction. Christian nationalism holds that if we do not restore ourselves to a Christian nation, God will judge us—while believing the world is destined to be destroyed.

As historian Thomas Lecaque wrote in a *Washington Post* opinion piece in 2020, "The Trump administration has left its apocalyptically inclined evangelical allies in an eschatological bind: They have an apocalyptic leader and an apocalyptic scenario, but they themselves are fully in power . . . or at least they have been."[21]

A kind of dispensationalist evangelical confirmation bias comes into play—a tendency to interpret culture wars and current events through a lens that best supports our assumptions. For example, present day sexual ethics or increased instability in the Middle East can create fear that the world is ending—and reinforce that only some of us have our eyes open to the right worldview. Some dispensationalists saw President Trump as a sign of the times because of the bias that already exists.

Bias is holding hands with its partner, control. If evangelicals are in political dominance, we are not underdogs with a particular, cloistered view of the world's trajectory and near end. If America can be "made great again," maybe America can be blessed again. Maybe disaster can be averted. Like a modern-day Nineveh.

There is a grave danger in building the church as an institution with political ties that bind. When leadership in the American evangelical church takes the role of savior through its political allegiance, there is no health or growth toward a true servant King. If the church swaps the posture of caretaker of brothers and sisters in Christ with that of gatekeeper—handing out membership cards to others who believe America is blessed—it becomes its own shadow, a new partisan political action committee that shows up at prayer breakfasts and stump speeches with American flags and wooden crosses.

Presidential Prophecy

While allegiance to the Republican Party was simmering well before Jerry Falwell launched the Religious Right in the 1970s, conservative white evangelicals normalized dispensationalist theology through the twentieth century—and politicians paid attention.

During the first of his two terms as California's governor, Ronald Reagan was quoted in a 1968 edition of *Christian Life* magazine as saying, "Apparently never in history have so many of the prophecies come true in such a relatively short time." A few years later, in 1971, he said of a coup in Libya, "That's a sign that the day of Armageddon isn't far off . . . everything is falling into place. It can't be long now."[22]

The press reported on Reagan's apocalyptic narrative while he was campaigning for a second term ahead of the 1984 presidential election. His connection with conservative evangelicals was scrutinized in national media; in a televised debate, Reagan claimed his apocalyptic interest didn't impact his policy and instead was "philosophical."[23]

Nationalism and dispensationalism worked hand-in-hand to fight against the threat of communism and socialism during the Cold War. Conjuring up Cold War imagery can strike a chord with premillennial dispensationalists like Dad, who read the book of Revelation in a "literal" interpretation, waiting for the "great king of the north" (interpreted to be Russia) to strike.

The Berlin Wall fell in 1989, and the Cold War officially ended in 1991 when Mikhail Gorbachev handed power to Boris Yeltsin. But the frenetic energy from some American evangelicals taking a defensive posture to protect democracy and religious liberty did not burn off.

Instead of rallying around an external threat, at the end of the Cold War some citizens began to refocus inwardly, to threats of liberalism and demographic shifts within the American population. Today, for the first time in the history of America, more elected officials are younger, female, nonwhite, and of various religions, including Muslim.

American unification in the Cold War worked like an immune system, developing a healthy resistance to communism. But by no means was the cause of protecting democracy purely noble. Think McCarthyism and the Red Scare.

Autoimmune disorders can attack our own bodies and fight our immune systems. Internal factors that led to Christian nationalism that came to light in the Trump era—including growing income inequality, America's demographic shift to a majority non-white population, and our online interconnectivity—have caused some of us to turn against each other.

Always Remember

Depending on who held office, evangelicals have interacted with presidents between Reagan and Trump by approving, ignoring, persevering, or complaining. Evangelicals generally supported George H. W. Bush. Bill Clinton's Monica Lewinsky scandal was fuel for a sustained and intense distaste for Bill—and especially for Hillary. Y2K, another notable event during Clinton's term, did not crash all computers from a coding error that would have thrown our systems into the apocalypse, as some dispensationalists predicted would happen. Society did not break down, American currency was not devalued, and the supply chain was not severed.

George W. Bush was generally approved of by evangelicals. A year into his first term, on 9/11, Americans watched footage of President Bush receiving the news of a plane hitting the south tower of the World Trade Center while he was reading a book to second graders in a classroom in Sarasota, Florida. That night, I would sit crisscross applesauce, packed in with other twentysomethings in a friend's living room in Muncie, Indiana, praying for protection over the Muslim students in our breadbasket community. No one knew if it was the end of a tragic day or the beginning of a very long war.

On September 12, the convenience store, liquor store, and most every fast-food restaurant in Muncie put up some mix of "We Will Not Forget" and "God Bless" on their signs. My friend Erica and I drove around town and took pictures. I could not articulate my feelings of experiencing 9/11 in a small Indiana town, but the signs were striking, and I only knew to document them. I did not have language for Christian nationalism. Only fresh grief for New York, ten hours away, where I'd lived the previous two summers.

The Arby's displayed "Let Freedom Ring" under their lit-up sign that looked like a giant cowboy hat. The liquor store sign read "God

Bless America" right under its usual all caps message: "KEGS KEGS KEGS." There was also a feeling of goodwill and tenderness in these God-and-country messages: sending support and solidarity in a common vernacular. The United States seemed to be split open and held together, near and far, by three words: God bless America.

By the time Barack Obama was elected in 2008, the political atmosphere in the country was still polarized—but in urban cores and other pockets of the country, the air felt electric. Hearing "Yes we can!" at rallies and reading signs with the campaign slogan "Hope" became unifying for many Americans, including the 26 percent of evangelicals who voted for Obama in 2008 and 21 percent in 2012.[24] Of all issues, evangelicals most aligned with the Obama administration on immigration, health care reform, and education.[25]

Hal Lindsey's predictions of a rapture in *Late Great* did not come to pass. Still, from Carter to Biden, Dad has held firm to his belief that Jesus is returning soon. Somewhere along the way, he stopped assigning as much weight to specific date predictions by leaders in the eschatology community. Dad voted for Trump the first time because of abortion, but he was in chemo during Trump's second election and didn't cast a vote. He told me he "could honestly not care less" who won, but he hoped to have someone "pro-Israel" in the Oval Office.

A Call for Pluralism

American demographics are changing. The country's population includes citizens from many nations practicing every religion or no religion at all. Attitudes about culture wars and politics between younger and older generations are often in contrast, as are different geographies that impact our beliefs, including the rural-urban divide.

At the same time, a 2021 Pew Research Center report found that instead of hemorrhaging members who were driven away by President Trump's behavior, the white evangelical church grew from 2016 to 2020. According to the report, more Americans started to identify as evangelical during Trump's presidency than stopped identifying as evangelical.[26] The Trump presidency drew people to evangelicalism instead of pushing them away. Instead of this statistic offering hope for healthy church expansion, it is a marker of dubious growth grounded more in political rhetoric than devotion.

Democracy is built on pluralism. In order to move toward a more perfect union, Christians are called to welcome diverse interests and beliefs, not simply to tolerate them. Pluralism cultivates a space in society where it is OK to believe different things about God and to love each other across those differences. No matter how much you believe in your own cultural identifiers, pluralism creates a society where there is space for others to organize their lives around different core beliefs, and for those choices to be respected.

Christianity is not defensive, and Christians do not need to take a defensive stance against religious pluralism. Separation of church and state is a key ingredient in pluralistic society—an ecumenical safety net that democracy should continue to protect. Any person claiming a Christian identity who sees diversity of belief as a threat is revealing a hierarchy of priorities that may well place country—in particular the conception of "country" as a place of white normativity—in front of God.

The Christian story upholds human dignity and leads with forbearance. There is no border of separation between the heart and the hands. The work of the cross does not cling to a personhood that "others" people in the service of dominance or control.

Setting the Scene for Conspiracy Theories

The Christian identity of nationalists, both stateside and overseas, may not be particularly Christian after all. As political and cultural commentator David Brooks writes in a *New York Times* opinion piece,

> Many of the so-called Christian nationalists who populate far-right movements on both sides of the Atlantic are actually not that

religious. They are motivated by nativist and anti-immigrant attitudes and then latch onto Christian symbols to separate "them" from "us." In Germany, for example, the far-right group that aggressively plays up its Christian identity underperforms among voters who are actually religious.[27]

The far right conspiracy theory group QAnon is a case in point. Adrienne LaFrance wrote in *The Atlantic* in 2020 that QAnon "may be propelled by paranoia and populism, but it is also propelled by religious faith." Or at least religious imagery and vernacular. "The language of evangelical Christianity has come to define the Q movement," she continues. "QAnon marries an appetite for the conspiratorial with positive beliefs about a radically different and better future, one that is preordained."[28]

In addition to dispensational evangelicalism, some aspects of New Age spirituality can lead followers to conspiracy theories and support of far right political stances. British philosopher Jules Evans researched the link between New Age practice and Nazism in Germany in the 1920s and 1930s, and he parallels Hitler's aura of inevitability for some Nazis to Trump's for some of the American electorate. Evans writes,

> Numerous Germans compared Hitler to a magician, a hypnotist, a medicine man, who cast a spell on his listeners in his rally speeches. . . . His followers attributed occult powers to Hitler of insight, prophecy, and infallibility, much like the more fanatical followers of Trump suggest he is playing "four-dimensional chess," so that even his misspelled tweets contain occult wisdom.[29]

From the pagan-tinged distortion of Christianity used by the Nazis to far right groups today, Christian imagery can easily be distorted to propagate messages of hate.

Hitler and his fellow Nazis sold the German people a simplistic supernatural fantasy and conspiracy theory, in which all their problems were caused by a hidden global elite of monsters/vampires/demons—that is, the Jews—but the magical light-warriors of the Nazi party would defeat them in a cosmic battle, ushering in a golden age of peace and love. . . . Doesn't this sound like QAnon to you?[30]

Being a premillennial dispensationalist does not make someone a conspiracy theorist. Dad, for example, scoffs at QAnon supporters like he scoffed at worshipers at the Toronto Blessing, the Canadian revival that began in a Vineyard church that made headlines in the '90s. Still, some evangelicals conflate a bloated and literal interpretation of the last days with conspiracy theories. Professor Charles King argues that the particular evangelical worldview that elected President Trump

traffics in conspiracy and encourages distrusting one's own eyes and ears. It substitutes idiosyncratic interpretations of ancient texts for questioning engagement guided by real experts in languages and history. It is beholden to charismatic leaders who combine consumerism, celebrity culture, and stadium-level entertainment.[31]

QAnon was not a big jump from premillennial dispensationalism for some evangelicals. Both dispensationalists and modern conspiracy theorists tend to pick apart information—be it Bible verses or current events—to decipher clues about what's to come. Like wiping fog from the windshield instead of waiting for the defroster. With a little more work, clarity will come—along with its sibling, control.

The influence of conspiracy theories on some evangelicals leading up to the 2020 election is striking. A 2021 American Enterprise Institute poll found that a notable 67 percent of white evangelical Republicans said the statement "an unelected group of government officials, known as the 'Deep State,' were working against the interests of the Trump administration" was "mostly or completely accurate," compared to 52 percent of Republicans who did not identify as evangelical. In addition, 31 percent of Christian Republicans affirmed that the following sentence is accurate: "Donald Trump has been secretly fighting a group of child sex traffickers that include prominent Democrats and Hollywood elites."[32]

It is a great irony that some white evangelicals feel like cultural minorities in an increasingly diversifying American population where people of color are shifting the vote—and shifting the face of Christianity. Some white evangelicals have warmed up to conspiracy theories and nationalism in response to changing demographics.

Ideologies which, if slapped together and put into practice, would result in a totalitarian government clamping down on individual expression and personal liberty.

As noted in a Berkley Center essay by international affairs scholar Tobias Cremer,

> QAnon, proud boys, and the like seek to repurpose Christianity as a cultural identity marker of white America. They parade Christian crosses at rallies, use Crusader imagery in their memes, and might even seek alliances with conservative Christian groups. But such references are not about the living, vibrant, universal, and increasingly diverse faith in Jesus Christ that is practiced in the overwhelming majority of America's churches today. Instead, in white identity, politics Christianity is largely turned into a secularized "Christianism": a cultural identity-marker and symbol of whiteness that is interchangeable with the Viking-veneer, the confederate flag, or neo-pagan symbols.[33]

In some churches, pastors preach from stages that double as podiums for visiting politicians. It's common to read social media messages from evangelical leaders endorsing certain candidates or disparaging others.

For many Christians in various generations, the melding of the church with Americanism is deeply personal. For example, a lot of us have navigated difficult stories of division in families and church communities after loved ones refused to comply with public health guidance, even if that meant unknowingly spreading Covid.

Revelation Is Not American

Christian nationalism doesn't just look like violent insurrection. It is a belief system that can manifest publicly, from the pulpit, and behind closed doors.

We cannot "Make America Great Again" when America was built on a broken system of white dominance that suppresses the freedom and well-being of people of color. This dominance was built on oppression, and oppression is abhorrent to God.

Much of the white American church has been complicit, but the way of Jesus is one of full redemption, offering conviction, forgiveness, and reconciliation. The upside-down kingdom brought a brown-skinned refugee king out of a manger. Can anything good come from Nazareth?

The error in Christian nationalism isn't the belief that God works through nations but rather the belief that God is uniquely concerned about the prospering of the United States more than any other government or country. God works in people groups and nations all over the world. God is concerned with the flourishing of all creation and people throughout time and geography. All who have come before us and will live after us are valued by God. The gospel spread for almost 1,800 years before the United States existed. If the gospel story is true at all, it must be true for every person and place and time.

The belief that God has special love for America is unorthodox and not biblically grounded. It's nationalism, with or without violent protests. And nationalism is idolatry. It adds an extraneous and erroneous label to the gospel that reflects the image of white Americans. Instead, the gospel is a message of love and hope for every person, created by God. For all cultures and times throughout history, in our present moment, and in the future.

Shortly after the 2020 election, I watched a lecture with *The Color of Compromise* author and historian Jemar Tisby. He called out Christian nationalism as a great current threat: an ideology that conflates Christian identity with American politics. "Justice takes sides," Tisby said. "You can't play the middle between right and wrong."[34]

Many American Christians, from all generations, believe that America is better and democracy is upheld when all creeds, colors, religions, and beliefs are made welcome. Our shared vision for the church is the vision of Revelation, one reclaimed from the version told to us by dispensationalists who look at the future through a filtered lens of Westernism, beginning with the Pilgrims and continuing through the Religious Right.

The prophetic book of Revelation is not American. Our liberation is not in making predictions for the future but in emptying ourselves of any cause except God's cause. Jesus says in Matthew 10:39, "Whoever finds their life will lose it, and whoever loses their life for my sake will find it." There is something beautiful in our poured-out differences rolling down the long slope of the holy mountain.

A Picture of Belonging

The Bible is a picture of belonging. Revelation shows us that people from all tongues, tribes, and nations will come and worship the God of justice. This picture looks a lot more like the reality of American demographics than the fever dream of Christian nationalism with its vision cast on a white ideal that was never inclusive or reflective of the God of all creation.

Today, the big heart of Jesus is beating loud in weary believers. His heart can transform families and faith communities divided by politics. This possibility of conviction and radical forgiveness is real, because the Christian life is rooted in Jesus's liberation and in his care for the oppressed. The liberation of Jesus changes people. And it brings people back.

This transformation Jesus brings is not reactive or defensive. Jesus was pressed on all sides in his time on earth. He was executed by political forces. Yet Jesus forgave and welcomed, praying for the very people who crucified him. Instead of building a fortress to protect the few, the American evangelical church can model the humility and sacrifice of its namesake.

CHAPTER 8

Work of the People

I f the transformation Jesus offers is rooted in belonging, it is established in practice. We all live out liturgies, all the time. I was raised hearing about the end times and culture wars around the dinner table. I was also raised on a weekend liturgy of watching TGIF sitcoms on Friday night, roaming the mall on Saturday, and attending church before passing spareribs around a lazy Susan at a Chinese restaurant like the one Dad ate at on Sundays while growing up with his Jewish family. I was raised on a liturgy of six television screens in a seven-room house, plus portable ones for the tub and road trips. I was raised listening to the "Bible Answer Man," "Focus on the Family," and John MacArthur's radio shows.

The word *liturgy* translates to "the work of the people."[1] It is the pattern and rhythm by which life is lived and faith is practiced. Liturgy is not just the stuff of smells and bells for high church folks. While I was growing up, my family had our work, and yours did too. Our work was American work. It was Christian work. Our work was to hand out tracts, which we kept in the glove box, when we got the chance. Our work was to not get "wacky" or "woo-woo" about how God moves in the world. Our work was mostly done alongside people who looked a lot like us. Our work was white and middle-class. Suburban and candy-colored. Our work was done in spandex—'80s leg-warmer Jazzercise work. The calorie counting book was next to the Bible. The Superbowl Shuffle came after the Sunday sermon.

Spiritual formation anchors Christians so that our liturgies can remain rooted in Jesus—not the market, not Republicans, not Democrats, or any other political party. Formative practices can infuse us with wisdom and perspective, so our faith is steadfast and does not become defensive or entwined with false constructs including nationalism, premillennial dispensationalism, or conspiracy theories.

Our spiritual formation begins in childhood. Whether nurturing or abrasive, factors we could not determine cast a shadow or a glow on our earliest understanding of God. However and whenever our faith journey began—in want or plenty—there is full agency in Christ to pursue formation with all our heart, strength, soul, and mind. Your parents or mentors may have been end-timesy like Dad, or not. Maybe you weren't raised with parents. Maybe you had a parent or caregiver who was plenty busy working to pay rent, without margin for directly engaging with culture wars. Or you weren't raised in a home where Christianity was practiced.

Maybe you are a person of color raised in a church community that looked very different from a cookie-cutter white church. Or you had a parent who stayed in bed for days straight like my friend's mother, held horizontal in a cloud of depression. I'd walk past her room with its door cracked open and quickly look away.

Each of us navigate our own layers of complexity from our families of origin, and Christianity may be a joy or pain point from our childhood. Sometimes our parents change as they age. Other times they die still holding the same view of the world and their place in it. Sometimes their conviction remains firm or stays stuck on a certain teaching or theology. For Dad and me, it always comes back to the end of the world.

Healing, over Donuts

Dad doesn't think about death like I do. Instead, Dad thinks about being raptured.

One night after his diagnosis, I imagined an exquisite death for myself, but Dad is the one who is dying.

I spontaneously combust on a holy mountain. Just bursting into flames but not really *dying* dying, more like floating up in embers. Kind of like Dad.

I wondered what it would feel like to be Elijah in an angelic chariot of fire, or to go from a mountain to being raised into heaven, until I was too sleepy to think anymore.

Dad has told me since childhood that God doesn't really heal people anymore. That even though it's OK to pray for healing, the gift probably ended with early Christians who used healing to spread the gospel. Unsurprisingly, I want few things more than to witness a healing. And I mean a dramatic healing: to see someone lay hot hands on another person until their gravelly breathing clears, their bones shift under skin, or their tremors still.

Dad surprised me one morning when he said he was healed while he was in the hospital. He told me what had happened while we were eating donuts. We'd mostly spent time together on drives to chemo until then, so that day we went to a bakery by a fancy outdoor mall. "At my lowest point, when I was filled with fifteen pounds of water, and I couldn't move, I wanted to die," he told me between bites. "And then at the lowest point in my existence, I just held both hands straight up in the air, and I said 'God, you said if I ask anything in your name, you will do it. I'm asking you, in your name, to be healed.'"

He said he turned his head toward his window, on the top floor of the hospital, and saw a small cloud all by itself in a clear sky, just sitting there. "Immediately, a ball as bright as can be passed through the cloud. I saw it dissipate. I never watched what happened to the ball afterward, I was so completely freaked out," Dad said.

"Was the ball the moon?" I asked.

"It was not the moon. It was a bright ball that went right through a small cloud," he said. "I turned my head praising God and thanking God for the miracle. I still don't know what happened to that ball."

I couldn't help but laugh a little. Dad was heavily medicated in the hospital, apparently enough to not know the moon. "It was not my imagination. I was not dreaming," he said, doubling down. "It was an absolute, genuine miracle, and it may be the only one in my life and the only one I'll ever have."

"But why do you call it a miracle if you still have cancer?" I asked him.

"That was God's decision. The cancer has made me into a different person, given me more confidence in myself, made me trust Jesus more. It's made a difference in people's lives."

I asked him, "So, it was more a spiritual miracle than a physical one?"

"Physically, I'm going to suffer," he said. "I'd rather not be sick, but I'm OK with it."

When Dad was talking, I thought back to a *Fresh Air* interview I heard in 2006 with Reynolds Price. It stayed with me, because it's uncommon for NPR to air a story of Christian healing. Price, a late writer and professor of English at Duke, talked to Terry Gross about his spinal cancer. In the hospital with a grim diagnosis, he had a vision of Jesus, who was standing knee deep in water. Price waded in and stood next to him. Jesus said, "Your sins are forgiven." Price asked Jesus, "What about my cancer?" And Jesus said, "Oh, that too."[2]

Christian doctrine teaches that the body and spirit are not able to be separated. That God cares for our physical, mental, and spiritual health. But in listening to Price's account of healing, I realized that Jesus often begins whole-person healing with the heart. In Matthew 9:2, Jesus encountered a paralyzed man lying on a mat and told him, "Take heart, son; your sins are forgiven" before telling him to pick up his mat and walk.

Dad said he needed a spiritual healing as much as a physical one. He prayed and saw a glowing moon cloud, something mysterious and strange. God met Dad, and Dad's eyes changed after. That night, without any particular intention or strategy, Dad experienced God in prayer.

Prayer, the beating heart of formation.

Inward Definitions

Spiritual formation involves disciplines to strengthen our faith in order to become more like Jesus. Finding structure helps us not just grow but be pruned to bear sweet fruit.

My pastor once talked in a sermon about spiritual formation being like a trellis, a structure that guides vines and flowers. Growing in the Christian life happens more easily with a framework to help us to mature: rhythms and practices of prayer and service, some done in solitude and if possible some done in community. Otherwise it will become harder to find our bearing as we grow.

It's difficult to objectively identify our own place in culture while we're living in it. The pursuit of spiritual formation allows us to see the failings in our heart and be shaped by the culture of Jesus. A growing spiritual formation, no matter how fast or slow, is an elixir for anyone whose heart tends to worry, fixate on hot button issues, or center on ego. In other words, most of us.

Culture wars and ideologies like Christian nationalism look to the external world to find enemies and threats. But as Christians define our identity inwardly, through a deepening and growing relationship with Jesus, we find health. The promise of hidden, inward transformation is gorgeous hope.

American Christians are a tiny corner of the church today, a bedroom community outside a great city. The church is thriving in emerging nations, with two-thirds of Christians residing in the Global South.[3] America is far from the first nation to have trouble separating culture from Christian faith. In the early church, Greeks struggled to separate broader societal beliefs from their identity in Christ. Instead of nationalism, gnosticism—the idea that the body is inherently bad and the spirit good—was infused in the church.

During my youth, evangelicals who read headlines about communes becoming cults and were suspicious of the New Age movement were tepid about the idea of exploring and teaching their kids about spiritual formation. Instead of getting fancy with liturgy, I was taught to simply read my Bible during a daily quiet time, which reinforced the biblicism of evangelicalism—Catholic practices, including monastic prayer and liturgy, were performative.

While spiritual formation is ecumenical, Jesuits developed deep formational practices that have informed much of the tradition today. The rise in popularity of spiritual disciplines aligned with historically Catholic practices led to a tepid reception by evangelicals who questioned the eternal salvation of people who prayed to Mary or went to a priest to forgive their sins while sitting in a stuffy confessional box.

Dad was used to taking an "us versus them" posture in culture. He was waiting for Jesus to return while some friends thought he was crazy. In my family, it was also natural to draw the line between Protestants and Catholics. If we'd met any Greek Orthodox families, they'd have been on the other side of the line too.

Plus, no one knew much about contemplative Christian practices. They weren't part of the zeitgeist. Instead of a rich practice of using liturgy and listening prayer to form a foundation that could withstand a changing culture, I was fed vacation Bible school curriculum and Christian summer camp songs around the fire that burned out after the weeklong programs concluded.

With no adaptive framework that grows with each generation and maintains relevancy, stories about Jesus can easily become nostalgia. The flame of "on fire for Christ" youth rallies will burn out if young perceptions of Jesus are not set up to grow with emerging minds.

Some of my Gen X peers who left the church did so because the church didn't look or feel like us. Some who stayed until after we were out of our parents' house or college bubble eventually left because we had not learned how to flourish as Christians in the wide world—where a lot of white evangelical families lived identically to everyone else.

Friends who came of age in '80s and '90s American evangelicalism moved to cities, started careers, and began families. We shared a common experience: cultural assimilation, as Mark Sayers and John Mark Comer talk about in their podcast *This Cultural Moment*.[4] The Missional church era I encountered in the early 2000s featured sermons with *Matrix* red pill/blue pill analogies and Sunday night services in bars that looked very different from my parents' church.

Inside Mom and Dad's nondenominational sanctuary, mauve pews matched mauve carpet. A capped hot tub rested behind a screen and served as an occasional baptismal. To appease older members, an 11:00 a.m. modern worship service designed to attract young families was launched after the 8:30 a.m. traditional service that stuck with organ-led hymns. Seasonal wreaths flanked both sides of the stage along with festive flags. When attempts to maintain relevance fizzled, churches like these began to lose the attention of younger members.

A Christian Spy and a Sea Change

My own spiritual estrangement led to a wandering that lasted twelve years. I was drawn to the city and to a church culture that was different from what worked for my parents. Naively, I thought I could change the city, when really it changed me. Quickly.

You should have seen me at Victrola, the coffee place in Capitol Hill we'd walk to after church. I did not carry a Bible. I did not wear a cross. I did not dress for Sunday. I just looked like a typical twenty-something wearing a vintage dress and ordering an Americano.

In my mind, it was impossible to live in the city and be a Christian, because I'd never learned how. I was a Christian spy. I was undetected as I stood by the cream and sugar station. In those years, I worked very hard to manage the image of my faith in the city, which surfaced as an awkward self-consciousness.

I moved to the Pacific Northwest to help start a cohousing community that ended after two years. I witnessed friends beginning to shed our shared evangelical identity. Those years broke apart my certainty about what I believed about God. My experience was common for the time, with intentional communities and house churches across the country flaming out in that same era.

It took years for me to slowly retreat from protecting my own reemerging identity and find a way back toward Jesus.

The spiritual reconciliation that knitted my belief about God together after more than a decade of lukewarm faith—and assimilation into a spiritual but not religious culture—flourished through a new approach to spiritual formation.

I began to explore Ignatian spirituality through Debbie Smith Tacke, who was on staff at my church as the director of spiritual formation in the late aughts, when more churches were beginning to weave in contemplation and listening prayer. I found my 1978 copy of Richard Foster's *Celebration of Discipline* and discovered the classic themes remained fresh. The book highlights inward practices, including prayer and fasting; outward disciplines, including solitude and simplicity; and corporate disciplines, including worship and celebration. "The need to change within us is God's work, not ours," Foster writes.[5] Slowly, imperfectly, moving toward several of these postures became the trellis that grew my faith. One of these practices was participation in Quaker clearness committees.

In 2017, my husband, Drew, and I considered moving back to the Midwest after living in Seattle for more than thirteen years. We talked for hours about every aspect of the decision. We outlined each scenario on 11x17 pieces of paper and wrote on both sides. We talked to friends about the decision. We waited. And, ultimately, we remained stuck.

Debbie recommended gathering a few folks from our church to form a discernment group inspired by a Quaker clearness committee, a process to move toward clarity about a central question or decision. I'd been a part of a clearness committee led by a Jesuit priest in a discernment class in grad school and valued sitting in a small group by candlelight and asking prayerful, open-ended questions to a classmate. I didn't realize how vulnerable discerning out loud can feel, but with help from the group, after a series of meetings, we discerned that we should stay in the Northwest.

The decision to become rooted in Seattle brought a season of grief for the choice we didn't pursue. But it also felt like removing a hair shirt or taking weight off my neck and shoulders. I learned through the process that a discernment about moving was more about calling than place, more about identity than geography.

Debbie and I also talked about applying Ignatian indifference to a central discernment question I was carrying about vocation. This Jesuit idea of "indifference" doesn't mean we don't care. Instead, Ignatian indifference is an active and healthy detachment from a decision, person, or experience. In my life, it looks like coming to an open-handed posture in front of two sides of an idea or choice and being willing to let one or both things go if they do not bring me closer to God's purpose.

To better love and follow God, we can pray to interact with what helps us flourish and release what doesn't. This framework has changed the way I think about discernment questions and helped me move from quick-tempered reactivity to healthy detachment.

When we're spiritually formed to practice applying a holy indifference, we can better extend grace to people in our lives who vote on the opposite end of the ticket. We can even disagree with fervor while loving each person God loves. We can release ourselves from balking, from knee-jerk outrage, and, at least once in a while, we can hold our beliefs with a looser grip.

Working It Out

In practice, spiritual formation is an inoculation against faith infiltrated by culture wars for three reasons.

1. Spiritual formation helps us hold fast to the Christian life.

Christianity calls all political and social systems into account, including our own. Becoming shaped by historic Christian faith and the witness of Scripture sets us on firmer ground to identify the brokenness of American culture—and to offer a prophetic word of challenge with the intention of being a healing presence in our world. Formation strengthens our faith and puts it in the context of a bigger story.

If it's a stubborn faith, a frustrated faith, or a deflated faith, we can still hold on to it. We can bind ourselves to it, even if in some seasons of life we are the oil and faith is the water. Engaging in the structure and rhythms of spiritual practices in the very midst of a flared, withering, or stagnant faith can carry us and hold us fast.

Our faith is supernatural, but it is also reasonable. There is a long line of Christian intellectuals, scientists, and social workers. Our faith is embodied, but it is also yoked to a wild Spirit.

2. Spiritual formation prevents us from being manipulated.

Our discernment muscle is strengthened through formative spiritual practices. Whether we're voting for a candidate for the school board, watching an ad for a wellness product featuring a celebrity, or listening to a sermon, learning to prayerfully recognize how we receive messages and ideas helps to inform our decision making and reveals our true inner motivations.

Metaphorically, are our hands open or closed around our political allegiances and buying patterns? Discernment helps us check our spirits well before ideas skew toward actions that are contrary to the teachings of Jesus yet covered by a veneer of Christianity.

Christian nationalists, for example, talk about being concerned with protecting religious liberty and personal freedom. But we don't grow by protecting. We grow by being anchored to what is true and lasting through formation. This posture of prayer, fasting, listening for God, tithing, serving, and bearing all fruits of the Spirit is true liberty and freedom.

It is not American nationalist freedom, which is shorthand for white-dominant, Republican-ruling homogeny. Nationalists have not been able to decenter faith from politics and they conflate pride in America with the construct of a white, American God they have created to serve their own interests: an anti-Christ to protect their tribe and keep the rest at bay.

It's as dangerous to succumb to cultural Christianity, a faith expression that goes through the motions but does not bear fruit, as it is to nationalist Christianity, a faith motivated by politics and power. Cultural Christianity may be more insidious because it is inseparable from capitalism.

Instead, the Christian life calls followers of Jesus to move from infancy to maturity. As Paul writes in Ephesians 4:14, "Then we will no longer be infants, tossed back and forth by the waves, and blown here and there by every wind of teaching and by the cunning and craftiness of people in their deceitful scheming." True freedom in Jesus is an anchor for the soul. When we are tethered to Christ, we can withstand not just personal afflictions and suffering but also cultural tides.

Formation surfaces unexamined biases. When we are pruned for fruitfulness, we will not bend when a movement tries to sway us with lies so clever they sound like a truth we want to hear.

3. Spiritual formation connects us to a faith rooted in love, not defensiveness.

In order to move away from cultural and political forces that seek to maintain the status quo or protect people in power, we need a destination to move toward. Formation leads Christians to the narrow path of Jesus and aligns their hearts to a rich faith tradition.

We live during a time in history when American culture wars are fought by using difference to stir up division. Culture wars can make us afraid of changing demographics or tell us to be defensive. Yet spiritual formation can free us to apply wisdom and intentional detachment to the way we choose to engage with, not hide from, our shared world.

In Mark 12:32–33, Jesus tells a scholar of the Torah that it is most important to love God and to love our neighbor.

> "Well said, teacher," the man replied. "You are right in saying that God is one and there is no other but him. To love him with all your heart, with all your understanding and with all your strength, and to love your neighbor as yourself is more important than all burnt offerings and sacrifices."

The scholar understood, and Jesus tells him he is not far from God's kingdom. No one in the crowd dared to ask anything else. This moment was a distillation. Jesus does not use a parable here. He says it plain.

These instructions—to love God and neighbor—are a knife and a magnet. A knife because the words cut clean through. A magnet because if we are to love and not self-protect, it must mean we are created with the innate capacity to be loved.

The Arrival Fallacy

The *arrival fallacy* is the belief that if we can achieve a desired outcome, we will find happiness. Harvard psychologist Tal Ben-Shahar uses the term in his book *Happier: Learn the Secrets to Daily Joy and Lasting Fulfillment.*[6]

I moved from one arrival fallacy to another throughout the pandemic. *If I can just get the vaccine, it will be ok. If my kid can get the kid vaccine, we will maybe be ok.* The dot on the horizon I moved toward was always receding.

Maybe there's something healthy in the idea of the arrival fallacy, a way we can be motivated to move ahead. In pure form, it is hope. But the problem comes when we think we'll find piles of diamonds and pearls at some just-ahead destination. A clamshell we can swim to on the horizon, pry open with bloody knuckles, and string its pearls on our necks. Drink the salty nectar and float back to shore.

Spiritual formation brings awareness to seasons of both desolation and consolation in our spirit. When we move toward God's love, we can be met with consolation. Happiness is not a requirement of this state of being. In fact, it is possible to be met and filled with God's love and peace in consolation even as we face a dogpile of afflictions.

Consolation nudges us to remember that God is good. If we don't trust in God's nearness and goodness, our anxiety will always keep us stuck and searching for the next arrival fallacy.

Here is where my feet are caught in the net, with questions like, *How is God near and good when nothing is getting better? How is heaven real and not a self-management tool, the ultimate self-soother of the mind, after more than six million people died of Covid? Can free will be this vicious?*

At my lowest moments, it seems God is nearer in daily superstitions and magic genie prayers for parking spaces than in my inner life. Yet while holding questions, even deep and wide ones, I believe that in the end all things will be made new. I do. I always have and probably always will struggle with these questions. I hold conviction for restoration in one hand like a fragile peach, and the weight of the pit in the other.

The Ordinary Hard

Some of us might experience or witness a physical or emotional healing, or some spiritual manifestation in our lifetime. But many of us wake up tired, pour a second bowl of cereal, and read the news. Most of us see and experience nothing miraculous.

Christians are spiritually formed in the middle of otherwise unexceptional days as well as in trials. Thank God for mystery and thank God for boring life too. Our minds sometimes think big and wild thoughts, and other times think about grabbing another snack.

The reality of spiritual formation is that it happens in the "ordinary hard" of life. Any kind of training, be it learning a new language or building endurance to run a marathon, is about developing the muscle memory and easy automatic response that can enable us to persevere and grow when we encounter the stress of real-life complications.

Blinding Light

When we are catechized by American culture, we learn for it to feel natural to vote for our own self-interest. But as Christ transforms our lives, we are compelled to take an outward posture toward community and service. The true witness of the gospel means giving up our own rights in order to care for others. Even the ones who hit a nerve at the holiday table.

Surely, formation is a lifelong thing. Luke 10:27 says, "Love the Lord your God with all your heart and with all your soul and with all your strength and with all your mind." Here, we are invited to pursue a clean heart and a liturgy of love that reaches beyond our own household. We are invited to turn our love for all that is created, and all we create, back to God.

The thought of it—to continue to be formed with that sort of love and let it change us—brings visceral hope.

Spiritual formation begins by choosing not to disavow what we can't see. There is something so wonderfully out of control about believing in a God we can't prove. Some might call it foolishness, a need to explain what happens after we die to cope. Others could call it anti-intellectual, narrow, and embarrassing. But I call it radiant. I call it abundant, transformative love. All color that seeps into a blinding light of love.

PART THREE
CONSUMERISM

CHAPTER 9

American American

F ort Wayne, where I grew up, is in the middle of a circle of Rust Belt cities. In a few hours we could drive north to Detroit, south to Indianapolis, east to Cleveland, or west to Chicago. Fort Wayne was named after a general, "Mad" Anthony Wayne, who was known for his blistering temper. Wayne established the town after pushing the Miami Tribe out of the region.

The city of about 250,000 people is sandwiched between commercial corn and soybean fields. Developers began to break ground on subdivisions in the 1950s, during a postwar boom felt throughout the US economy. But as I was growing up it had become a brick city with emptying factories as blue-collar jobs continued to move overseas.

Fort Wayne has several tributes to the general, including the Mad Anthony Brewing Company and a foreboding statue in Freimann Square, the main park downtown, that was restored and rededicated with better lighting and landscaping in 2014.[1] It's a sobering truth that many American generals have been commemorated in towns across America for inhumane acts like Wayne's.

The statue in the center of town may have been restored, but my own childhood home a fifteen-minute drive away looks like a ghost of itself. What happens to the places we loved when they're gone? Or worse, when they've fallen apart? For some of us, along with church, home is an embodiment of both nostalgia and grief. Our roots and heritage. What we left behind with the leaving. The feeling that even though we're long gone, we can't quite be free.

The suburban ranch house where I grew up looks smaller and in greater disrepair each time I'm in town and drive past. It was foreclosed several years ago. I found the online listing, which read with too much literal sadness to be ironic: many new updates were completed . . . in the past. An inventory of everything in the house followed, as if it was to be broken down and sold for parts: Shower. Back patio. Linen closet. Pantry.

I stuck a small green sticker from the Christian bookstore of a praying Jesus on the linen closet, where it stayed for years. A cartoon God that brought some strange comfort when the lights were out. My mother let me paint part of the interior door of the pantry when she was doing a touch-up, which I blotched and smudged. It's probably still there, rough and wrong.

White Bred

Evangelicals have drawn a hard "us versus them" line in culture war issues like abortion. But when it comes to the market, there has been an unquestioning assimilation. One clear microcosm of American consumerism white Christians have embraced instead of pushing back against is the growth of the white evangelical church within the growth of suburbs.

Racism, suburbia, and church expansion have been formative factors in the rise of the evangelical church in America. Understanding discriminatory practices that led to the whiteness of the cul-de-sac after World War II, and the suburban experience in the 1980s and '90s, reveals areas for the church to repent and consider a new way forward rooted in plenty instead of scarcity.

About sixteen million Americans from the Greatest Generation served in World War II. These military service members were incentivized to move to the growing number of housing developments in the suburbs by subsidized mortgages from the 1944 GI Bill. This bill offered low-interest business and home loans. Working with the Veterans Mortgage Guarantee Program, the Federal Housing Authority issued loans to both home developers and buyers. Interest rates beat those of banks or private lenders, and families began to move to new housing developments outside of cities.[2] A third of Baby Boomer families had secured suburban addresses by 1960.[3] Churches followed the growth, breaking ground in the suburbs and increasing American church membership between 1950 and 1960 from 49 percent to 69 percent.[4]

In *The History of White People*, Nell Irvin Painter recounts the story of literary critic Louise DeSalvo, whose family left Hoboken for the New Jersey suburbs after the war. DeSalvo writes that her mother started buying commercial white bread instead of home-made loaves, because, in DeSalvo's words, "Maybe my mother thinks that if she eats enough of this other bread, she will stop being Italian American and she will become American American."[5] A Jewish company, Levitt & Sons, developed Strathmore, one of the nation's first suburban developments on Long Island, but Jewish families were not allowed to live there.[6]

My mother is Italian and my father is Jewish. Both sides of my heritage were late to join the fold of who were considered to be "white Americans." My family stood in line after families with ancestors from Ireland, Germany, and Eastern European countries. We were slow to become "American Americans," in spite of our white skin.

In the 1930s, the federal Home Owners' Loan Corporation generated "Residential Security" maps of cities across the United States to determine mortgage-lending risk levels used by real estate and home appraisal professionals. In total, 239 cities were color-coded, from green to blue to yellow ("definitely declining") to red.[7] Residents of redlined areas were typically Black, Catholic, Jewish, or Asian. Red neighborhoods were deemed "hazardous" credit risks, and loans to improve homes and businesses in these communities were restricted.[8]

"To be American American had quickly come to mean being 'middle class' and therefore white," Painter writes, "as in the facile equation of 'white' with 'middle class.' It was as though to be the one was automatically to be the other."[9] Because of housing discrimination, Black families were prohibited from moving to the suburbs for decades. Covenants that restricted Black residents' access to suburban neighborhoods remained legal until 1968, when the Fair Housing Act passed. By that time, appreciation had made the purchase price of suburban single-family homes unattainable for many families of color. The suburbs were occupied by white families when they were built and stayed white for the decades to follow.[10]

Racial discrimination continues to impact neighborhood demographics in both the suburbs and the city. In Seattle, Rev. Dr. Samuel B. McKinney, the late civil rights leader and pastor of one of the city's oldest Black congregations, Mount Zion Baptist Church, told the Seattle city council that five banks denied his loan application to build a new church sanctuary. He said the experience was

> just another attempt, we felt, on the part of white system to try to keep black and other poor folks from trying to achieve their dreams. . . . We didn't know it was called redlining, all we did know was when we went to the bank to get a loan we couldn't get it.[11]

Given the ramifications of Black exclusion from purchasing property, it's instructive to consider the striking generosity of communities of color. Black philanthropy, including church tithing, accounts for $11 billion in annual giving to charity. A 2012 study from the W. K. Kellogg Foundation and Rockefeller Philanthropy Advisors found that Black households donate a quarter more of their annual earnings than white households—more, in fact, than any racial group in the United States.[12]

Housing discrimination does not just reflect neighborhood demographics. It also reflects the kinds of churches planted in urban or suburban neighborhoods, and who attends them. Some storefront churches founded by pastors of color initially meet in community centers before expanding into a space in a retail area. In contrast, suburban megachurches are often built from the ground up on enough land to be called a campus. A 2020 study reported that while the ethnic background of megachurch attendees is increasingly mirroring American demographics, 94 percent of senior megachurch pastors are white.[13]

At best, rapid suburban church growth after World War II is evidence of congregations opening their doors to support new communities flush with school-age children. But suburban church expansion in that era was impoverished by its omission of congregants of color, instead forming insular populations of members that looked like them and lived in a similar way.

A New Center of Gravity

From 1945 to 1955, $4 billion was spent on new churches in the United States. Many of these buildings were constructed in suburbs like mine in Fort Wayne. The post–World War II baby boom resulted in a large generation of white kids, many of whom were raised in rapidly expanding suburbs with parents who belonged to a local church.

In *Witnessing Suburbia: Conservatives and Christian Youth Culture*, author Eileen Luhr writes that "during the post–World War II era, the suburb became the new demographic center of gravity in the United States."[14] Here, families could experience social growth, ideally alongside spiritual growth. However, churches "focused on the social aspects of their congregation to the detriment of doctrine and theology," and Luhr names examples of how church became as much community center as house of worship,

> with child-friendly amenities, extensive programming, and coffee hours. This form of "popular religion" focused more on morals and patriotism than on "ecclesiastical religion," which adhered to rigorous institution building, traditional rites, and formalized doctrine.[15]

American evangelicalism grew whiter with the suburbs. And as the suburbs served consumers, consumerism was happy to be of service to the church. Luhr writes,

> To conservative suburbanites, the protection of the white middle class entailed not just home values but values in the home. Their views reflected the suburbanization of American evangelicalism, a belief system well equipped to address within a consumer idiom the private concerns and emotional needs of families.[16]

Some Boomers followed a spiritual curiosity to a different faith tradition, agnosticism, or atheism. But many Boomer Christians attended an evangelical church, opening the bottom of a Dutch door to a Sunday school classroom for their kids filled with books, curriculum, and ephemera from the local Christian bookstore.

Responding to an expanding market in the '70s and '80s, Christian media and parachurch organizations grew alongside suburban populations of church attendees. A handful of small cities or suburbs near larger urban cores became the headquarters of evangelical organizations, including Colorado Springs, which is home to Focus on the Family, Compassion International, and Young Life.

Christian media also established a presence in the suburbs. A 1978 *New York Times* article dubbed Wheaton, Illinois, a "corporate Christian ghetto," listing the organizations and evangelical businesses based in nearby Carol Stream, Illinois, including Tyndale House publishers, Youth for Christ, and *Christianity Today*, "a conservative and literate weekly that had been based in Washington."[17] The article can't help mentioning how

> most of the executives do business at lunch time in the Hamlet Restaurant, the best in Wheaton—except that it is strategically situated outside the city limits, so that those who like to do business over a drink can do so. The city of Wheaton has been dry since it was founded by Methodists a century ago, and it is not likely to become

wet now that it is known as the town where Billy Graham went to college.[18]

Acid Heads

Boomers entered adulthood at a tumultuous time in American history. Tom Wolfe coined the Boomer moniker "Me Generation" in a classic 1976 *New Yorker* piece. In the article, Wolfe mentions the evolution of some hippies into saved Jesus People. "At the outset practically all the Jesus People were young acid heads, i.e., LSD users, who had sworn off drugs," who "had suddenly made religion look hip."[19] He claims Boomer hippies ended up with a faith that looked a lot like their elders, with an edge.

> Without knowing it, many heads were reliving the religious fervor of their grandparents or great-grandparents . . . the Bible-Belting lectern-pounding amen ten-finger C-major chord Sister-Martha-at-the-keyboard tent-meeting loblolly piny-woods share-it-brother believers of the nineteenth century. The hippies were religious and incontrovertibly hip at the same time.[20]

An edge of "hipness" began to wear off later in the 1970s, and many Jesus People settled into the suburbs like their parents. In middle age, hippies moved from peace, protest culture, and self-exploration to suburban security, establishing house and home—in homes that happened to look a lot like each other.

Boomers continued to read grim headlines, including Watergate and economic upheaval. Tens of thousands of lives were lost in the Vietnam War, which finally ended. As photographer and writer John Bassett McCleary put it, "The 1970s have been described as a transitional era when the self-help of the 1960s became self-gratification, and eventually devolved into the selfishness of the 1980s."[21]

The '80s saw Reaganomics grow the economy and beef up the military while slashing the social safety net. Robin Leach ended each episode of *Lifestyles of the Rich and Famous* by sending us "Champagne wishes and caviar dreams," and Michael Jackson turned into a werewolf on MTV. That's where kids like me came in.

Plentiful Amenities

As a generation of evangelical Gen X and older Millennial youth came of age in suburban congregations, church remained a social center point. But as one Black friend shared, his earliest experiences of prejudice and discrimination came with the pressure to assimilate in the white evangelical church. Being a person of color in a predominately white congregation required bearing the weight of racist undertones before he experienced them anywhere else in his community.

In sharp contrast to my friend, I participated in this church world gladly. I dressed up as an angel and stood on the bleachers to sing "Hark! The Herald Angels Sing" at our church's "Walk-Thru Christmas" every December and enrolled in vacation Bible school on the lawn in July. I got a new outfit and sat with my parents for Olan Mills photos for the church directory. I pledged allegiance to the American flag and the church flag each week in Sunday school.

Church may not have infused me with spiritual formation, but it was social. I made friends and had crushes. Church was the place I went after cereal and a little TV on Sunday mornings. Church was where I learned to recite books of the Bible in alphabetical order and memorize verses. These practices were good for me. They were structured and regular. But they did not help me articulate how the Christian life should look or feel different from regular American suburban life.

While plenty of people from my youth group ended up leaving Christianity, some of my peers experienced a positive differentiation from their parents and remained anchored to faith. I can quickly think of several friends who have remained Christians in part because of a healthy grounding in childhood from a parent or mentor.

When asked what their parents did right, my friends say the same thing: nothing special. Their parents were not desert ascetics or pilgrims walking the Camino de Santiago on summer break. They were simply not rattled.

One friend saw his mother read the Bible and pray, in the same chair, at the same time, most mornings. Another benefited from long talks with his father, who welcomed questions and fostered a casual sense of spiritual curiosity. A third had a parent who was a pastor and saw how joyful that calling could be. These people, living with intention and formed by ordinary trials, modeled Eugene Peterson's words; the Christian life is "a long obedience in the same direction."[22]

Yet I saw few people convert to Christianity in my childhood. I do not recall anyone answering the altar call at church except one week, when a man in recovery from alcoholism publicly asked for prayer. The air was electric that Sunday, and I wondered how down on his luck the man must have been to request prayer in front of so many families for something that I figured was better left a secret.

Mostly during that weekly altar call, I just felt bad for our pastor, who stood there Sunday after Sunday, facing the pulpit and singing a hymn with the rest of us. I was embarrassed that he had to stand there alone, because maybe he felt like he was failing God—or worse, us, his congregation. I almost went forward myself once, just to keep him company, but never got up the nerve.

A Lot of Stuff

At church, there was often an imaginary line between youth and adults. As my peers and I inched closer to adulthood, the tradition and structure of Sunday services did little to orient our hearts toward Jesus. Youth groups for teens were up against hormones, after all. Jesus stayed a character in an illustrated children's Bible instead of a God who could transform our lives and change the way we saw other people. With the exception of some teen-centric service events, we were not called to live differently.

Church occupied one day a week, and the other six were filled with ample TV time in our wood-paneled family room. I was raised on sitcoms spliced with advertisement jingles that stuck in my brain far more than three points in a sermon. Author Ada Calhoun writes in *Why We Can't Sleep,*

> Gen X has been described as both repulsed by materialism and deeply materialistic, and there may be something to that. Those of us whose formative years were the 1980s were steeped in a bath of greed and gluttony: the yuppies' BMW and Armani fetishes, sports car posters, *Wall Street*. We may have rebelled against it later by buying secondhand clothes, but we're inculcated, deep down, with wanting a lot of *stuff*.[23]

We went to the movies, bought clothes at The Limited and Express in the mall, and swung into the car dealership to lease a new sedan every two years. We went out to eat at Cheddar's and ordered the giant chocolate chip cookie in a cast iron pan for dessert.

We talked less about Jesus and more about everyone else not being into Jesus. Prayers were brief, though sometimes beautiful and earnest. My family did often talk about Bible verses at home, though usually either in the context of a culture war issue or about Jesus returning soon.

Eventually, Jesus was going to come back, and cut off the good stuff like a strict parent: Jesus was your mom telling you the playdate is over right before you were going to ride bikes. Jesus was your dad giving you an early curfew after you finally got your license and wanted to see a band play in the city.

So I ate the giant cookie while I could, and I ate it with ice cream and hot fudge.

Nevermind

When the Berlin Wall fell in 1991, we ordered a piece from a TV advertisement. The small hunk that arrived disappointed me because there was no spray paint on it. It could have been from any rock pile in any pocket of the world. I saw the images of young Germans climbing on the wall on the news, through the fuzzy screen, arms in the air. It was nighttime in Europe. Dad talked about the wall falling and what clues it could offer for the end of the world.

The fallen wall brought unity and openness; Berlin was a whole city. And for me, a teenage kid in Indiana, 1991 was also a year when everything shifted. As the world was changing, my body was changing. There was an inevitability to growing up then, as a white suburban kid at the start of the 1990s. Later that year, at a middle school sleepover, like millions of peers I'd hear Nirvana's seminal *Nevermind* on compact disc for the first time.

My church was a ten-minute drive from home, near subdivisions with names like Walden, Blackhawk, and the Lakes of Buckingham. But on the Sunday after hearing Nirvana for the first time, my mind was two thousand miles away in Seattle. It would be years before I'd arrive, but I knew then I was going to live in the Pacific Northwest someday.

Gen Xers like me were defined more by what we questioned than what we believed in. At least that was how we were portrayed in the media. And like it does for all cultural moments, the media both created the narrative and fed off one that already existed. My peers and I were not emotionally wired to respond positively to seeker-sensitive churches that welcomed Boomers. When we were old enough to legally drink, we checked out churches in pubs. We tried intentional communities inspired by Shane Claiborne's New Monasticism, with its call away from the individual and toward community. We put up Celtic crosses and lit candles on stage at the Sunday evening service.

Postmodernism was a concept some of my evangelical college classmates feared. "'God is dead,' Nietzsche / 'Nietzsche is dead,' God" posters were common additions to cinder block dorm room walls. The worry on campus of a looming threat to God looked like a giant shadow on the wall that really came from a stuffed animal.

Postmodernism was woven into other new concepts in undergrad philosophy classes, like Derrida's deconstruction and aesthetics, the philosophy of beauty.

I left small-town Indiana for Seattle with several friends in the early 2000s. We wanted out because every main drag in middle America looked like a carbon copy of the next, with the same big box stores and chain restaurants, but we felt infinite. No one talked about our access to infinity, the white privilege of our wandering. I didn't admit it to anyone, but I found comfort in the thought of plopping down on my parents' overstuffed furniture to watch the wide screen if the city didn't work out.

Such lifestyles are a choice, and choice is ultimately at the heart of consumerism. Consumerism tells us to live in the city or move away from it or gentrify it. To make art that's weird but still commercial enough to sell. To find a microcosm of people like us and preach to the choir. To want to be famous, or at least social media famous, but not talk about it.

Consumerism is vacant, because it is about serving the ego of self, and there is a spiritual hollowness that comes with it. There is no nutrition in a supersized life. We always have room for seconds.

It would be a long time before I would understand the sweet fruit that can grow when you stay in the place where you've come up. I didn't look beyond the Walgreens and RadioShack to feel a pull of the raw beauty of the land in northeast Indiana. *Moving to the city means leaving forever*, I told my young self. I was following the general bent toward urban ministry.

Inspired by Tim Keller's work at Redeemer Presbyterian in New York City, young Christians talked a lot about serving the city in the early 2000s, and more churches began to plant congregations in the middle of cities to meet demand. A reverse migration.

I didn't think about gentrification and assumed my presence could be nothing but an asset to any city core. Here in Seattle, my friends and I could have learned a lot about grounded presence and direct service from the historically Black congregation at First

AME, a church that had been serving the community surrounding Pine and Madison for 125 years. But we did not ask. We were brand-new, following a bread crumb trail that led us to prewar walk-ups, espresso carts staffed with baristas who'd played in grunge bands back in the day, and long walks with peek-a-boo views of the Space Needle from the lookout over I-5.

Shifting Demographics

Discriminatory practices in housing may have been legally banned by the Fair Housing Act in the late '60s, but housing discrimination and redlining are still reported today.[24] Demographics are shifting again—the 2020 census confirmed that America is more racially diverse than at any time in history, and the suburbs are getting more diverse.[25]

As white families return to the city or move farther into the country, people of color are populating suburbs due to job opportunities and increased affordability—and as a result of gentrification. Yet instead of an embrace of diversity, segregation persists in the suburbs. Nostalgia has a pull that is not inherently good or bad, but not everyone has experienced what white suburbanites may miss from the past.

Whether they are lacking in empathy or simply uninformed and disconnected from communities of color, white evangelicals have historically denied, downplayed, and politicized the influence of systemic racism. Instead, a veneer of ecumenical worship that messages an openness to diversity and "color-blindness" is perpetuated. There are an increasing number of voices that have been lifted since the murder of George Floyd in May 2020, but within white evangelicalism there remains a generalized ambivalence to the need for the white church to participate in deep racial reconciliation.

Fear was at the root of white flight from the city, and the church has too often not been a countervoice of love but instead succumbed to anxiety and presumptions that led to self-preservation. The church is meant to be of every color and creed but instead has held a posture of scarcity, hoarding its abundance.

Yet the gospel message speaks to a homegoing. God is preparing a place for us. In heaven we will be part of

> a great multitude that no one could number, from every nation, from all tribes and peoples and languages, standing before the throne and before the Lamb, clothed in white robes, with palm branches in their hands, and crying out with a loud voice, "Salvation belongs to our God who sits on the throne, and to the Lamb!" (Rev. 7:9–10)

It's forward-thinking, the biblical idea of our forever home. It's not an image of ranch houses that break down over decades and grow back wild. There are no red lines on maps but seats at one endless table. Our true home is a place we long for, a place we know we're going even though we've never seen it.

CHAPTER 10

Gold Teeth

When the Jesus People movement ended and its communes disbanded, New Age and Eastern religions began to capture the imagination of Western culture, causing some in the church to overcorrect with a focus on literalism instead of mercy.

Like other evangelicals of my generation raised in the suburbs, I was a late bloomer to contemplative Christianity. That's partly because liturgical practices like the examen and lectio divina have only started to gain more traction in Protestantism in recent years, as my peers began meeting with spiritual directors and scheduling silent weekend prayer retreats. I was also so late to discover the richness of the contemplative tradition because I was raised to be suspicious of any spiritual practices that mixed evangelicalism with Catholicism.

When I was growing up, Dad said Catholics were crazy to think they were drinking the literal blood and eating the physical flesh of Christ during communion. Communion bread and wine were safest in the form of a dime-sized paper wafer and a small swallow of grape juice. The Catholic belief in transubstantiation—the doctrine that the Eucharist actually transforms to the body and blood of Christ after it is consecrated by a priest during mass—was too much like magic.

There was little that was spiritual about my church experience growing up, and I craved real substance. Bread and wine would have been a start. Today, most spiritually curious folks don't see church as a viable option, because in many instances the American evangelical church is not very spiritual. Eastern religion, yoga, sound baths, and vision quests are visceral, experiential, and, honestly, more spiritually in tune than a lot of American Christianity. That's why many modern Christians are looking toward liturgy and high church traditions.

I want the mystery of the leavening, and all the imagination I can bring to communion. The bread raises the spirit and the wine burns through any fog hovering over the heart. Our friend Pat used to hold the bread in a communion circle and say, "This is the body of Christ. Go ahead, take a big piece."

The Holy Spirit is yeast. The Holy Spirit is a vitamin. All restoration and growth, working through pinot or grape juice or Kool-Aid; challah or Wonder Bread or saltines. I don't care so much about the form. I care about the communion line joining all Christians together, the joyful and the weary, all those who came before and those still to come. Let it be a little dangerous. Go on. Take a bigger piece.

A Hot Slice

In addition to a suspicion about mysticism and the spiritual realm, I was raised believing that Catholicism did not center on Jesus but instead was caught up in ritual, and its adherents prayed to saints and Mary instead of only Jesus. One extreme was experience, the other ritual.

Catholic practice, Dad reasoned, may not have been *technically* blasphemous, but parishioners were clearly not interested in a literal interpretation of the Bible. Catholicism added a lot of toppings to the pizza, and hungry evangelicals like us just wanted a hot slice on a paper plate. The sinner's prayer was brief and clear, while Catholic practices of penance, confession, and purgatory were fat that needed to be trimmed.

As opposed to Catholicism, which introduces people into the church sacramentally, through baptism, at the heart of Protestantism is a central individual conversion moment. Unless you're a kid who comes up evangelical, in which case you might tend to question if you're really saved. In a similar frequency to my "Jesus is coming back . . . now!" game, I repeatedly asked Jesus into my heart at night when I was a child, seeking assurance to tamp down my anxiety.

Guard Your Heart

I was taught that the end of the world would come with an actual rapture in our lifetime and, paradoxically, that I would not see the gifts of the same Spirit of God manifest in healing or prophetic prayer. Dad's focus on a literal interpretation of the Bible led to a deemphasis on spiritual gifts and a general suspicion of the Holy Spirit working in everyday life. We were to guard against "opening ourselves up" to the spirit world.

When we can't predict how or when we might experience the spiritual realm, good or bad, it's natural to want to put all spirituality in a locked box that can be explained using propositional logic that can be systemized and understood. But this kind of understanding can be a means of trying to control God.

Manifestations of the Holy Spirit remind us that we are not in control. That's why a literal interpretation of the Bible has been so important to Dad. Some Boomer evangelicals like Dad have a fear of unbridled spirituality, lumping the New Age movement in with Pentecostalism: reading tarot cards and being slayed in the Spirit are on an equal playing field under this logic. Ironically, watching for the end times encourages premillennial dispensationalists to scan the headlines for signs and wonders.

Spiritual formation was not understood let alone practiced in my church circles. Instead of engaging in contemplative practices, we spent time outside of Sunday services deadening our sense of spiritual impoverishment by buying stuff we didn't need. Be it virgin piña coladas from Red Lobster, plastic charms for necklaces, or an early rendition of a giant flat-screen television that took up half of the living room wall.

Dad filled any possible space for healing, contemplation, or direct service with stuff. Batteries, Scotch tape, tweezers, and Big League Chew. When it is healthy, gift giving is his love language. But gifts can quickly become excesses, a way to fill his time and load up the junk drawer with wintergreen Lifesavers. Dad buys extra incidentals for a reason. It's a compulsion to anticipate needs instead of the alternative of leaving margin for want.

My parents padded our lives with an abundant amount of stuff, blocking pathways for spiritual vitality. By the time children of Boomers like me came of age, the path to a contemplative and vibrant faith was paved over with rituals of dressing in our Sunday best, attending youth group, and giving our cash to the industry of white evangelicalism.

Cessationism and Spiritual Gifts

Dad talked a lot about "God's will" for our eternal salvation when I was a kid. "Once saved," he said, "always saved." I bristled at the idea of an inescapable fate for much of my young adulthood, while ironically continuing to ask Jesus into my heart to cover my bases.

We listened to Christian talk radio constantly. While Dad loved John MacArthur and the Bible Answer Man, he was less interested in James Dobson and Focus on the Family's advice for raising me. Although he did buy me Dobson's *Life on the Edge* when I graduated high school in 1996—along with just about every other parent of every kid entering the Christian liberal arts college I attended. I still can't forget the chapter when Dobson lists his "12 steps to intimacy" using strategically placed all caps for emphasis. Stage 1: EYE to EYE moves innocently to stage 6: HAND to WAIST, and soon races to stage 10—giggle-whispered about by Christian teens from coast to coast—MOUTH to BREAST.[1]

Evangelicals agree on at least one thing: Jesus was physically raised from the dead. The resurrection is not a metaphor but a visceral, bodily occurrence. The old rugged cross was so real you might look at your thumb and find a splinter. But like many families in the Calvinist tradition, I was taught that certain spiritual gifts do not occur today, a belief called cessationism. Cessationism is a teaching that some "charismatic" gifts of the Holy Spirit that fell on early Christians at Pentecost—including healing the sick, prophesying, and speaking in tongues—ended with the first-century church in the apostolic age. Cessationists argue that those gifts were needed only to give the Christian message a sort of turbo boost, to gain traction and spread.[2]

It didn't make sense to my ten-year-old brain why gifts the Holy Spirit gave the early church at Pentecost would need to be returned. It was also unclear which gifts had continued and which ones had ceased. Dad was OK with safer gifts, like teaching. But he was especially wary of the relevance of the spiritual gifts Paul lists in 1 Corinthians 12:8–10:

> To one there is given through the Spirit a message of wisdom, to another a message of knowledge by means of the same Spirit, to another faith by the same Spirit, to another gifts of healing by that one Spirit, to another miraculous powers, to another prophecy, to another distinguishing between spirits, to another speaking in different kinds of tongues, and to still another the interpretation of tongues.

There were a lot of contradictions with some gifts that ended with the early church still rarely being allowed in specific circumstances. Like healing. As a child, I commonly joined in prayers for healing when a friend or church member was diagnosed with cancer. But other gifts of the Holy Spirit on the 1 Corinthians 12 list, like words of knowledge and especially speaking in tongues, might open us up to the devil and were for an earlier time.

The only books my father has read, besides *Late Great* and *Portnoy's Complaint* by Philip Roth (a universal rite of passage for adolescent Jewish boys in its era), were written by John MacArthur. He may have read a book after his cancer diagnosis and skimmed other titles here and there. But dad has read more than a few by MacArthur, a conservative evangelical pastor and host of a popular syndicated radio and television show. MacArthur has become an even more divisive figure in recent years, making disparaging comments on topics like race and the role of women.

When I was a kid, Dad tended to agree with most of MacArthur's theological positions, including his support of cessationism. Many Christians feel differently about this issue, and there are scholars who make a strong case for the relevance and timeliness of spiritual gifts. Spiritual gifts remain a charged issue in niche evangelical circles. For example, in 2015, a self-proclaimed prophet slipped past security while MacArthur was at the podium of his Grace Community Church in Sun Valley, California. The prophet's message to him? "You have grieved the Holy Spirit of God. Your doctrine of cessationism is an error. He has been grieved, John MacArthur. I've been sent here to tell you that."[3]

An Airport Revival

The sex and drug lore of hippie-born communes garnered headlines after the Summer of Love. For evangelicals who read about communes and watched them flame out by the end of the '70s—with some turning into cults first before flaming out—there was a draw to the materialism that grew with white middle-class families in the '80s. Cessationism was a belief that fit the time.

Some of my parents' peers chose instead to double down on spiritual gifts, attending Vineyard Fellowship churches, an offshoot of Calvary Chapel that split in the '80s over the Vineyard's heavier focus on gifts of the Spirit. Vineyard congregations blended conservative theology with "aspects of the therapeutic, individualistic, and anti-establishment values of the counterculture."[4]

Dad had no trouble believing that the return of Jesus would happen in our lifetime, but when we heard about a more charismatic interpretation of God reviving the church in the news, he would scoff.

He was dubious of the Toronto Blessing—a reported revival that began in 1994 at the charismatic Toronto Airport Vineyard church. According to the website of Catch the Fire (the church that began as the Toronto Airport Vineyard before becoming unaffiliated from the Vineyard in 1995), almost a million people from around the world visited their sanctuary during the first two years of the decade-long revival; the church self-tallied tens of thousands of conversions.[5] Lines stretched around the block that probably looked a lot like Seattleites in line for a scoop of cold brew cashew praline ice cream at Salt & Straw on a Friday night. Everybody wanted a taste.

One night, we watched a news report during dinner that showed grainy footage of a man crawling on all fours near the church's altar. "People walking on their hands and knees like dogs on a collar, people roaring like lions," Dad said, disgusted. "One guy said he was 'drunk on the Spirit' and literally looked like a slurring drunk preaching on the stage," he clucked, rolling his eyes.

Even though Dad scoffed at charismatic churches and reports of what happened in Toronto, by the time I got my license, he absent-mindedly greenlighted Friday nights spent at coffeehouses at the Fort Wayne Vineyard. Here, bands with names like Homeless Jesus and Puddle Jumper would perform in the dark sanctuary, sometimes giving an onstage testimony between songs. My friends and I went most weeks, even if we felt a little on edge about it. We once heard rumors that an exorcism had been performed in the hallway next to the sanctuary a few weeks prior. Some kid lay on his back, foaming at the mouth, while a pastor cast out demons.

Lorna Dueck was a young Canadian reporter covering the early days of the revival. In a *Christianity Today* article on the twentieth anniversary of the Toronto Blessing, Dueck recounted her experience.

"On those nights I was prayed for I spent a few hours of my own in 'carpet time,'" Dueck writes. "Carpet time" she explains, is "the Catch the Fire term for what happens when people are knocked down, 'slain in the Spirit,' and leave mysteriously strengthened and renewed in their love for God."[6] What would Dad have thought if he'd seen "carpet time," a phrase that conjures images of preschool naps?

Dad said news reports of miracles at the church were heretical fluff. On the other hand, he also said we would float in the sky and that dead people would leave their graves to join us during the rapture. Bones would turn from dust to frame to full, fleshy skeletons. Zillions of bloody, ticking hearts, dewy eyes, and beatific minds would lift up, up, up.

Reports of present-day miracles were unbelievable, but Dad's clear-eyed view of a mass resurrection of cinematic proportions was as practical as stocking up on grocery staples or going to an annual checkup. The rapture, practical and near.

Not much footage has been salvaged from that Toronto Blessing. A *Christianity Today* article from 1994, including interviews of both critics and proponents of the revival, reports, "recipients often begin to quiver, go limp, or fall. Others sob or laugh. Some lay in prolonged states of seeming ecstasy."[7]

Larry Norman played a concert at the Toronto Blessing in 1996, two years into the revival. Before beginning his first song, Norman delivered a long message to the crowd. "Your rent, your children's food, the money to repair your car or your teeth, it's there, it's on the path, it's in front of you, do not leave the path," Norman said, as the crowd began to softly laugh. I wondered, Is this holy laughter, or nervous laughter, or was everyone simply happy when Norman told them God would provide money for their dental work? "I just want you to remember one thing in your life," Norman continued. "It's short. It could fit on a bumper sticker." The crowd continued to laugh, and Norman said, "I'm serious . . . just remember . . . Jesus, good. Satan, bad." The crowd was exuberant.[8]

Ho-Ho-Holy Laughter

The Toronto Blessing's effect stretched across Canada and the United States. A 1996 *Washington Post* article with the ingenious headline "Filled with the Ho-Ho-Holy Spirit" includes interviews with worshipers at an Assemblies of God church outside of Seattle with members who had been overcome by holy laughter for up to several hours. According to the congregants, after people came to their senses, they described having experienced healing from past trauma. A pastor was initially skeptical about the revival. "I didn't want to turn into a cult," he said. "Then I found out about the healing. The laughter is almost an anesthetic while God does His work."[9]

Later in the article, holy laughter and Toronto Blessing critic Hank Hanegraaff disregards the phenomenon as classic mass hysteria.

> All of the manifestations you see in these churches are duplicated every day by B-grade stage hypnotists. It's basically mass hypnosis and auto-suggestion. There is peer pressure. . . . Their expectations are aroused, they've read about it in the Christian tabloids. And then there is the star status of the preacher. People work themselves up into an altered state of consciousness.[10]

I spent my adolescence hearing Hanegraaff's voice from the back seat of our family's car when he was known as the Bible Answer Man on the syndicated radio show he began to host in 1989. Three decades later, Hanegraaff's show was dropped from its evangelical broadcasting network when it was revealed that he had been confirmed into the Greek Orthodox church.[11]

Golden Hour

At one point during the Toronto Blessing, attendees reported receiving gold teeth; one account reported three hundred fillings turned from their original metal to gold. Some were shaped like a cross. There were also reports of gold dust; I found a video still of a mound of gold collected on a middle-aged man's Bible as he smiled and held the spine open.

A woman reported gold flecks appearing on her hands, which I recall seeing in a grainy old video. She claimed to have tried to wash the gold dust off, but it would keep reappearing. She started blessing other people, taking them by the hand and passing the gold dust gift.

Jesus, who rode a donkey over palms; a carpenter; the nomad preacher who ate with tax collectors; the servant king—two thousand years later—had finally turned everything to gold.

At the Great Commission, Jesus tells his friends,

> All authority in heaven and on earth has been given to me. Therefore go and make disciples of all nations, baptizing them in the name of the Father and of the Son and of the Holy Spirit, and teaching them to obey everything I have commanded you. And surely I am with you always, to the very end of the age. (Matt. 28:18–20)

The world is broken, and gold dust does not cover its cracks. A child who gets sick and not better, a global pandemic, the murder of a Black man who was running into a convenience store to buy a bottle of iced tea.

Our commission holds no guarantee of healing or holy laughter. Praying "God, do what you will" with full hope sometimes leads to a miraculous restoration and other times brings endurance for unanswered burdens. The Holy Spirit is a disrupter, moving outside of boundaries. This Third Person of the Trinity manifests in often unseen and only sometimes felt ways that come with unpredictability—even if that unpredictability is wonderful.

When God does not act, it is not because God is unkind, distant, or unable. Oppression and grief happen alongside moments of blinding beauty and grace.

"Blessed are those who mourn," Jesus says in the Beatitudes, "for they will be comforted" (Matt. 5:4). God created the world, and here we are in it—autonomous and free. Grace is the mystery of your story without a written end.

Wells, Not Fences

In recent years, and especially through Dad's illness, I've been learning how to pray in full faith for restoration while holding a loose grip on any desired outcome. "It wasn't God's will for me to get the job." Maybe you weren't the best candidate. "God wouldn't have willed me to get sick." Maybe, in our weakness we really are made perfect in the end, even when our bodies fail.

Christians are free to ask God to act in full faith. Sometimes that means persevering a little longer if God is silent. If God does not act when we want God to, or in the way we desire, our faith may be vulnerable—our hearts may turn a little counterclockwise and spiritual disorientation can set in.

That's especially true when navigating the pain of leaving a church home. Or the disappointment of visiting a new church with hope that it will be a place of belonging and community only to be rejected, be it for your gender, race, sexuality, physical disability, or not presenting as neurotypical.

Here is a call for pastors: build wells, not fences. An Australian farmer supposedly said that, after he learned to dig wells for his cattle so they could easily get a cool drink, instead of using gates to keep them on designated land.

My pastor John used this illustration once in a sermon to show the unanxious posture Christians can embrace. Instead of building fences to keep folks in the pews—a tactic rooted in scarcity and control—we can, like Pope John XXIII said, "Throw open the windows of the church and let the fresh air of the Spirit blow through."[12]

Jesus is the one who draws hearts that will be drawn. It's not our job to do anything except love each other well and serve each other before ourselves.

Before I was able to serve well, I had to understand a little about suffering. Many things in my own life have not turned out the way I'd self-narrated them in my twenties. I wanted to feel sad and true things in those days: the privilege of emoting. Reading the Russians, watching foreign films. Putting my own future into a series of complex stories that typically involved happily eating ramen on a blanket in some unfurnished city apartment, simply feeling alive, like my idea of Patti Smith and Robert Mapplethorpe making art at The Chelsea Hotel.

Real-life trauma is not melancholy-cool like a sad movie. There is no vicarious suffering when you and the people you love have been harmed by a person or institution claiming the name of Christ. It cuts. It weighs.

Instead of manifesting through an emotive spectacle, God is close in middle of the night ruminations. Jesus, with clear eyes, often works in quiet, away from stage lights and the merch booth, to bring consolation and hope. The Holy Spirit's presence can burn through any fog of grief and bring healing—no cloud of gold dust in sight.

CHAPTER 11

A Sea of Micro-Authoritarians

s a Christian, I feel an ongoing need to declare independence from the parts of the church that perpetuate brokenness. But, perplexingly, I'm fully dependent on God. In fact, I find freedom in that dependence.

It's surely a paradox to both declare independence as an individual and live with full dependence on God. I think of Matthew 10:39, where Jesus basically says, "If you cling to your life, you will lose it; but if you give up your life for me, you will find it."

In a 2016 PBS interview celebrating the anniversary of her seminal album *Horses*, Patti Smith talks about the opening line of the first song on the record, "Gloria." Smith sings, "Jesus died for somebody's sins but not mine." In the interview, she says those lyrics have been misunderstood since they were first heard in 1975. The song was a "declaration of independence," and the lyrics are not meant to disrespect the claims of Jesus, whom she considers an important prophet.

I first heard the name Patti Smith in high school, because I loved R.E.M. and the band's lead singer, Michael Stipe, loved Patti Smith.

Stipe famously sat up all night as a teenager in the '70s, eating a giant bowl of cherries and listening to *Horses* on repeat. "In the morning I threw up and went to school," Stipe told *Interview* in 2011.[1] There is risk and confidence in Smith's voice. Maybe, even as a kid, Michael knew intuitively that she was a visionary, that this music was not like anything else.

It might be a different album, travel, or a sports team. Whatever the vessel, many of us can relate to having a moment like Stipe's in which we declare a certain independence from our family of origin when we're on the way to forming a deepened self-identity. It's a developmental thing.

The desire for a lot of teens to leave their hometown starts small— a sudden desperation to run to the store for milk, loop the block on foot with headphones on, or do anything possible to escape the house in thirty-minute increments. I sat up plenty of nights (minus the cherries) with headphones, trying on different aesthetics and ideas. Poems were plastered on my walls, and Friday nights were spent in the poetry section of my local Borders bookstore. I read "Leaves of Grass" out loud one day without knowing what the words meant, except that they felt important.

I'd seen the Bible used like a decoder ring unlocking future se-crets. But as I began to read literature and learn about aesthetics, I thought about how God created the senses. How Jesus spoke in parables when he didn't have to. Realizing God cared about color, landscape, and story brought a new consolation.

The Allure of Authority

Jesus straightened tilted hearts in the people who submitted to his authority. But we're probably less interested in authority in present-day America, at least if we're Millennials, or a member of my Gen X cohort, who lean cynical and skeptical. The word *authority* may cause us to grimace; we may display a visceral reaction to phrases like "the authority of Scripture" and "church authority." However, the gospel calls us to decenter ourselves, including on social media. To get anywhere close, we're going to have to come to terms with authority.

Americans seek authority for a few different reasons. First, we're used to it. We live in a culture of deep-seated, toxic masculinity. It's common to hear US politicians use authoritative language on the stump. Narratives of the strong man resonate more loudly with some of us than others. President Trump is an obvious example of a person speaking with a form of authority many evangelicals were ready to hear. Trump sold himself as the powerful savior white American evangelicalism was waiting for.

Second, authority can be a helpful shortcut. Instead of taking a long time to learn a universal truth, we can turn to authority as a compass for a path we're told contains less suffering. Self-help books sell because they promise a faster way to solve our problems under the guidance of a wise influencer who already walked through it so we don't have to—and now they can share their life hacks or ten foolproof steps to reach a goal.

Third, authority is appealing because many of us crave being part of something bigger than ourselves. Participation in a movement with a compelling leader can bring meaning and belonging. Influencers often use common language to unify a group of people, be it a hashtag like #orphanedbelievers or the use of words like *reclaim* or *decenter*. This flavor of authority floats the possibility of connection and kinship.

Influencing and Being Influenced

Whether we're religious, spiritual, or none of the above, social media has a particular pull. Everybody has a pulpit, and some influencers secretly take pleasure in a hearty following and high engagement rate—in being an authority without being called one. In the recent past, commercial breaks between sitcoms sold products with familiar jingles, drawing a clearer line between advertising and entertainment. Today, influencer marketing has seamlessly woven its way into online content. The "sponsored" note on the top of an Instagram post is ubiquitous and easy to gloss over. Paid content is its own microeconomy.

In a 2021 *New York Times* op-ed, writer Leigh Stein compares a new flock of female Instagram influencers to televangelists of the '80s and '90s. Women celebrities, Stein argues, name-checking Gwyneth Paltrow, Brené Brown, and memoirist Glennon Doyle, are cultivating an on-demand church for millions of Millennial followers on Instagram, many of whom identify as religious Nones.[2]

At the time of writing this chapter, Doyle's memoir, *Untamed*, has been a *New York Times* bestseller for a full year. *Untamed* and books like it are a modern generation's *Late Great*. Both reflect their time. Lindsey's writing resonated with a generation reeling from Vietnam and the assassinations of MLK and JFK. His readers were bracing for a coming nuclear threat leading to an apocalypse.

Doyle's writing resonates with a generation of mostly women readers who were kids during Y2K and 9/11 alongside Sasha and Malia Obama. Lines in *Untamed*, like "This life is mine alone, so I have stopped asking people for directions to places they've never been,"[3] deeply connect with a generation raised in the pursuit of the authentic self. This message complements what those of us with doting parents heard as kids: we could be anything.

At least until the 2008 recession hit.

Wildest Dreams

As Millennials declared their independence, they were fed a steady diet of autonomy and self-empowerment through lifestyle. There was a smaller appetite for the corporate body of the church, because the way of Jesus demands a lessening of self for the sake of the body. In Matthew 10:39, Jesus says, "If your first concern is to look after yourself, you'll never find yourself. But if you forget about yourself and look to me, you'll find both yourself and me" (Message).

Millennials moved into adulthood, started careers, and learned that when they took a leap without a safety net, they sometimes crashed. Then they talked about it. Failure, vulnerability, and authentic self-exploration are rites of passage. The generational difference is how those things are communicated. As a Gen Xer, at times I feel more like a geriatric Millennial and often hold a tension between under- and oversharing online.

Ironically, we love authorities who preach about independence—but we're all following the same leaders. Influencers leverage messiness as *relatability*. We might believe we've become who we are without taking a hearty cue from others. That we are the answer we are looking for, and we've had the power to unlock freedom in our heart the whole time. *Eureka*.

I'd argue we are being sold self-empowerment. Because being the boss of us works—until it doesn't. The market, as usual, has responded by selling us the possibility of a just-out-of-reach authentic self, worthy of grabbing a green smoothie with our favorite influencer if the stars ever aligned. Independence comes at a price, and for many people, admission is too high. But we buy the conference pass or interactive planner anyway.

Independence can be and often is a beautiful thing, yet public figures like Paltrow and Doyle take it further to perpetuate a message that we are in control. How that message lands for Christianity is complicated, because there is a fine line between losing yourself and finding yourself. But if the authentic self is found through losing ourselves in the Christian story, consumerist culture is shouting the opposite, that our life is ours alone. Maybe we're hungry for a better articulation of self-identity and calling, to show our faces in good light. But without intention, we can move from therapeutic consumerism—buying stuff that makes us feel good—to perpetuating the myth that our wildest dreams for health, work, and love can be believed into reality.

Hyper-Agency

When we are denied agency, it is an assault on our dignity and humanity. But a focus on *hyper*-agency can quickly become problematic.

Early Christians proclaimed two things: Jesus is Lord and Jesus is Savior. Evangelicalism focuses a lot on how Jesus saves. We tend to talk less about what it means to proclaim that Jesus is Lord. That's because for many evangelicals, like many Americans, consumerism forms the rhythm of our lives.

The market can easily become a greater force of formation than Christianity, because consumerism tells us individual purchases, meals, and link clicks stack together to create an authentic life. Hyper-agency dangles a golden carrot of success on a string just out of our reach.

In health, the church calls us to community as our full, broken selves. The church has failed a lot of Christians, through scandal or abuse or nationalism preached from the pulpit. But some of us left the church because it did not fit with our personal brand.

According to a 2020 Pew report on the American religious landscape that Stein quotes in her op-ed, the 22 percent of Millennials who identify as religious "Nones" unaffiliated with any religion tend to push back against the church's teaching on political and social issues. They don't like organized religion and question religious teachings. Stein asks,

> Are we truly nonreligious, or are our belief systems too bespoke to appear on a list of major religions in a Pew phone survey? . . . Our new belief system is a blend of left-wing political orthodoxy, intersectional feminism, self-optimization, therapy, wellness, astrology and Dolly Parton.[4]

Some of the values on Stein's list, specifically self-optimization and wellness, thematically overlap with influencer content. She is identifying a common refrain that describes many spiritually attuned people who are searching for a new belief system. The church, flattened by culture wars, has done a poorer job of welcoming those searching than influencers and wellness experiences have done. But I'd argue the deep community of the broken, modeling the love of Jesus as best we can, is a balm we all need. That's because Jesus is the ultimate self-decenterer. He told people he'd healed to not talk about what happened until the right time. He shamed and humiliated himself, allowing himself to be stabbed in the side and hung to death in the open air.

This is not a failure for show. There would not be an Instagram influencer Jesus.

If Christians don't pair our buying habits and online personae with in-person compassion for our neighbors, we're just virtue signaling. There is little difference between a self-help influencer and a Christian driven by self-preservation and comfort. Many who do not identify as Christians deeply care for others in the expression of their social and political values. Anyone who decenters their own ambition to serve the poor and speak against injustice is closer to Christ than a cultural Christian.

In the Gospels, a picture is painted of Jesus trying to be obscure in crowds. His parables were unclear and dreamlike. Still, he became a phenomenon. People came out from the countryside in droves to see him. And a lot of them were there for the spectacle.

Jesus wanted people to follow him to the point that their own lives were turned inside out. In Luke 14:25–26, Jesus says, "If you come to me but will not leave your family, you cannot be my follower. You must love me more than your father, mother, wife, children, brothers, and sisters—even more than your own life!" (ERV). Such followers decentered themselves and gained spiritual friendship and embodied community.

Democratized Fame

It is a uniquely American irony that famous (or Instagram-famous) people become authorities, moving into a role of guide in our lives.

American authority tends to be earned on social media by tweeting something punchy that goes viral, singing through a vocoder, or looking hot in an activated charcoal mask.

Social media gives us a chance to build authority with or without accreditation, historical context, or prudence. The church of self is projected on the Instagram feeds of health-wellness-spirituality influencers, usually women, using the same template as inspirational coaches to encourage us. Deep down, we know the reasons these influencers are engaging with us are complicated and include a shaken and stirred concoction of both others-focused encouragement and their own career.

Stein, who is not religious, writes, "We're looking for guidance in the wrong places. Instead of helping us to engage with our most important questions, our screens might be distracting us from them. Maybe we actually need to go to something like church?"[5]

Social media influencers have democratized fame and made it populist. We're left navigating an online ecosystem of micro-authoritarians who are messy like us, have been there like us, and wear the same jeans as us. They are not the pastors of our youth.

Oversharing does not lead to virtue. There is no nutrition in self-curation. An online growth strategy can work up the elusive algorithm for a little while, until people get bored. Then our favorite influencer increases the number of wellness products schlepped in sponsored posts.

When we begin to sense that we're caught in the current of the market, maybe a little dissonance stirs up. The mythology of capitalism says we are the ones who make our own choices in a free and open marketplace. We are our own keepers and get to construct our identities by buying products and choosing the brand allegiances that make us who we are.

Is that how we treat religion now? (Do I sound like your granny yet?) We take some of this but less of that. We've been raised in a world that tells us we are allowed to decide for ourselves, and that feels good. A lot of us enjoy calling shotgun on independence in the market. We like self-reliance in decision making and the rush of satisfaction that comes when we think we're in control. Or at least I do.

Some of us go further. Maybe we want to keep unraveling and pushing away from Christian practice until the nebulous shape of something new is created. Maybe we want a world where there is no longer any organization disseminating information about the right way to live and believe.

Even if it is subconscious, maybe we believe that a living community can replace any religion that smells like mothballs and damp basements, that the cracks and crevices of our afflictions can be filled with the sweet sap of belonging to each other. That we can pull apart everything until a fresh, green shoot springs up.

We probably can. At least for a little while. But what I believe we can't do is create the life story we want without failing ourselves and each other. And none of us can make up a story more gorgeously decentered than the gospel story.

Instead of rebuilding ourselves, we can choose to decenter ourselves. This work is a magnet pulling toward the life and posture of Christ. Realizing we need to decenter because we're not the best authority of our own lives—hopefully before we burn out—can be incredibly destabilizing. Then it is totally freeing.

There are a lot of reasons we use social media, be it to find people who agree with us or vent at people who don't. To feel better about our bodies or worse about our bodies. To find a recipe or kill time clicking around someone else's online life. But the emotional and spiritual struggle is in the headspace. Some platform or another is on my mind, every day of my life.

Theologians such as Marva Dawn and Walter Wink would say all human organizations have powers at play—good and evil. Our allegiances come with emotions, and these can quickly spike. Take parents at a local school board meeting arguing for or against mask mandates during Covid. Look at who is or isn't elected to lay leadership at church. That's true in the social media space too. It's compelling to consider the spiritual dynamics at work in any public outlet. I've wondered a few times, Is there a power and principality connected to Instagram?

There is a clear performative aspect to social media that, whatever the form or fashion, tends to self-center. Church can be performative too. But I don't know if it's possible for social media not to stir up comparison, envy, or longing for an aspirational life that's just out of reach. Groundedness is often lost in translation from screen to screen.

Participating in online communities can be fruitful—it can keep us connected and curious. For some of us, social media can become a kind of spiritual community, at least for a season of life. Yet the core of Christian faith is embodiment, which only happens in our gathering together. That's why, although a gift to the immunocompromised like Dad, Zoom church during the pandemic felt distant for many Christians.

At its healthiest, social media can build beautiful communities and lasting friendships. But it is difficult to come together online compared to gathering as a broken body of people who are in each other's real, local lives. People we don't get to choose. For me, that's got to be the church.

Ecclesia Semper Reformanda

After decades of slipping in that I attend church or pray in hopes that I'd pass an imaginary test for my many agnostic and atheist friends, let me tell you: beliefs only get weirder to share the longer you wait. Not talking about my Christian identity makes me feel disingenuous and detached, like the most central thing in my life is the one thing I'm not talking about.

I also think there's another dynamic at play. If we withhold our Christian identity, we tacitly participate in the cultural narrative that we can manage or customize how we message ourselves. Perhaps we feel like we can direct an imaginary brand identity. I know, because I've tried.

Curating when or how to present our lives as Christians gives us a sort of control. But mysteriously, being a Christian means giving up on the idea that we can predict the outcome of our lives. As humans, we're complicated and messy, and reducing ourselves to a brand means we tailor everything to be on message. In many circles, Christianity isn't the best way to lead.

Here's another way forward. Instead of hoping folks pick up on an inferred message that we're Christians, we are absolutely free to humbly identify ourselves as people who believe in Jesus.

We have permission to call ourselves Christians. Even if that word is complicated. In the midst of the complication, I think it's the best word we have. I don't want the most nurturing and sweetest part of my life to be hidden, because that doesn't do myself or the church any good.

Again, many of us have experienced church abuse and hurt in particular congregations. Sometimes we need to step back, and sometimes that break needs to be extended. During a difficult season within a congregation, I felt the grief of broken leadership that cast a weight across the congregation and my own spirit. Grief was palpably on me, and I had to leave the sanctuary, sensing God more clearly in the fresh, clean air.

Still, church is not about meeting our own particular needs as much as it's about gathering together to worship God. Jesus didn't establish an individual, gnostic spirituality. He gathered an embodied community, and he left one behind after his ascension. A collection of broken people living life that remains two thousand years later.

The great, wide church is the body of Christ. The church binds together Christians before us, in our time, and to come. Each manifestation of Jesus, however big or small, however healthy or unhealthy, will remain, because the church is a piece of Christ's body.

It may feel hopeless. Discrimination by race, gender, and sexuality, as well as verbal, emotional, and sexual abuse inflicted on people seeking Jesus—all are bitter and broken reminders of the insidiousness of misaligned power. That is why it is more pressing and necessary to move toward a reformed, revived church in the very face of these abuses. Those of us who are safe to stay have a lot of reconciliatory work to do to restore the church as the Holy Spirit leads.

Ecclesia semper reformanda is a Latin idea that theologian Karl Barth popularized in the 1940s. In English, that phrase translates to "the church must always be reformed."[6] The white evangelical church has largely failed at its calling to "always reform" itself and come back to Jesus. Unless its failure has been part of its reformation, an arrow pointing toward a fresh start.

The Christian life is incomplete without the church. The deposit of faith—and the legacy of Jesus—only comes down to us through the church, as it has throughout the ages, including in seasons when the church is only a remnant as it regrows.

Even in this moment in church history, after Donald Trump earned the evangelical vote two times. After Christian nationalists stormed the Capitol praying for revival. After church leaders abused and continue to abuse power. In the presence of those in the church causing sexual harm, or who are complicit about the insidious racism in our past and present. All these things cannot keep us from Jesus's invitation to belong to a community of redemption.

When Christians decenter ourselves, we also decenter our congregations. We become less obsessed with influence and punchy messages. We can be unanxious about our faith and resist the call of the market telling us that Christianity is supposed to do something for us if we sacrifice for Jesus.

After all that has happened and all that will happen, in your life and in the world, your presence in Christian community is welcome and needed. In order for Christianity to flourish, it must be lived out, in practice, with other people. Otherwise the flame will be kept under the bowl.

Ecclesia semper reformanda. The church is reforming now because it must reform. There is room for all of us, broken and whole, estranged and at home, to rest in community.

Winter Citrus

If we're going to be small as we rebuild, church, let's be small. Let's go back to spiritual milk before solids, while looking for the swift work of the Holy Spirit to bring new hope and life. Let's winsomely preach the truth.

Jesus wasn't marketing or brand-building when he preached. He put the Christian message into the ether. Some listened but then left. Jesus, turning to his friends, asked, "You do not want to leave too, do you?" (John 6:67).

Some days I wish I could go, because I want to be on my own journey. But in my spirit, I know there is no magic, prosperous hand of God in cartoon form, waiting to #bless. There is no self-help manifestation of the Holy Spirit. Hard things happen to Christians just like everybody else. From time to time, the wonderful, terrible hand of God breaks down our spirits. And from time to time the enemy of our souls clouds our hearts and minds. Sometimes I don't want to be tested, tried, or convicted. I want to check out. I feel the attraction of *away*. I pray like the man who wept on his knees in front of Jesus, "I do believe; help me overcome my unbelief!" (Mark 9:24).

I am an American. I am a modern person. I understand the social capital it can cost to live in the world as a Christian. I feel the pull toward influencers and upward mobility in my own life—toward causing a ripple in a still pond. Toward filtering and framing how I talk about who I am and what I believe.

But the liberation that comes from pursuing a chosen obscurity—of living well without the need to be remembered and letting God be the God of your whole life—is ripe and sweet, like an orange in the middle of winter. Hold out your palm, ask for the wholesome fruit. Ask for help as you need it, all spiritual nutrition. The desire to soothe uncertainty by looking for answers from influencers and authorities may not stop. The diagnosis may not change. In our world, systemic oppression remains. But in surrendering to God's living love we find a wild, sweet orange. Faith that transcends. Vibrant, seeded hope.

◆◆◆

What if we embraced the weakness of being affiliated with the church?

Let me tell you, it can be isolating and alienating to sit at the table without any defenses. But here's why it's important to admit who we are: it's really not about us. And that's immensely liberating.

As Christians, we believe our lives are hidden with God, and to spend a lot of anxious energy skirting around that identity, for whatever reason, is tiring and kind of boring. God holds our identity, and we can stop striving. If we don't belong to the world, the least we can do is belong to each other.

As Christians, our great binder is Jesus. The one who claims radical and transformative love for the outsider and the oppressed. The one with a banner of hope over his breast. The one who, we find, comes to life in prayer and brings rest. When we embrace that identity in freedom, we can begin to be influenced by God's Spirit instead of our own ego.

If you're part of the ninety-nine, be grateful. If you're the one lost sheep, let yourself be gathered up.

Simone Weil said a daring thing: "Christ likes us to prefer truth to him because, before being Christ, he is truth. If one turns aside from him to go toward the truth, one will not go far before falling into his arms."[7]

It's a brazen idea, to be so confident in the reality of Christ that we can pursue truth with a full heart and mind, only fortified by any exploration. To wander with confidence that if the Christian story is true, we will circle back around.

When some of us leave the church or Christianity, we don't come back. But, be it fast or slow work, some of us can and will return.

There are a lot of dead ends in the flesh, a lot of wrong turns that can hurt us and each other. We are all swimming in a sea of micro-authoritarians. But if Weil is correct, if we seek truth with our whole heart, knocking on the door until it opens, and Christ is truth, we can be unanxious. If this whole thing is real, let it be real.

Isaiah says, "He tends his flock like a shepherd: He gathers the lambs in his arms and carries them close to his heart" (40:11). If Jesus is the good shepherd, let yourself be shepherded.

CHAPTER 12

Burnout and the Aspirational Class

I woke up early on a January Saturday and drove with my family from rainy Seattle to the Cascades to see snow. On the way, Drew and I talked about the loss of social currency that sometimes happens when you identify as a Christian, especially in an urban setting.

"I think most liberal, urban, 'aspirational class' folks are choosing against Christianity not because it isn't compelling but because it doesn't fit with their social identity," Drew said as we climbed elevation and reached the icy Skykomish River. "It's an albatross around their necks."

We started to wonder, Why can't there be room in culture for people like us, who live in cities, are centrist to progressive politically, and are earnestly drawn to Jesus and freed from the constraints of the "God and country" Christian stereotype that dominates the public narrative?

"Not just a one-dimensional straw man image of a Christian," Drew said, "but a person full of the contradictions and complexities that come with being human." We began to imagine what it would look like for Christians to embody a new, full identity apart from the majority of evangelicals.

When we talked about these ideas that winter of 2018, we knew less about the range of abuse being covered up within the church. We hadn't yet learned about the predatory behavior of church patriarchs like Jean Vanier and Ravi Zacharias, nor did we foresee the #churchtoo movement that began to uncover sexual abuse and harassment plaguing Christian churches. Before there were debates about mask mandates, before the murder of George Floyd and Black Lives Matter, before the 2020 election and January 6 insurrection.

Drew's question was posed with an optimism that has since been depleted. But the sentiment of the question remains the same. How do people who follow Jesus maintain our identity when the word *Christian* is complicated and holds implications? Now I see the depravity more clearly and understand the questions of identity with more nuance.

Workism

It's hard to spend time thinking about how to articulate your Christian identity in our complex culture if you have little margin. In 2019, Anne Helen Petersen wrote a viral *Buzzfeed* article titled, "How Millennials Became the Burnout Generation." The piece uncovered some of the systemic reasons why Millennials tend to work outside of the normal constraints of 9 to 5, blurring the lines between home and career and leading to deep fatigue.

"We have far less saved, far less equity, far less stability, and far, far more student debt," Petersen writes.

> The "greatest generation" had the Depression and the GI Bill; Boomers had the golden age of capitalism; Gen-X had deregulation and trickle-down economics. And Millennials? We've got venture capital, but we've also got the 2008 financial crisis, the decline of the middle class and the rise of the 1%, and the steady decay of unions and stable, full-time employment.[1]

The question of how work affects well-being is further explored in an *Atlantic* article on workism:

> The economists of the early 20th century did not foresee that work might evolve from a means of material production to a means of identity production. They failed to anticipate that, for the poor and middle class, work would remain a necessity; but for the college-educated elite, it would morph into a kind of religion, promising identity, transcendence, and community. Call it workism.[2]

Had work become a "religious identity" that replaced church? On a news segment for a Seattle-based NPR station, Petersen, alongside a local rabbi and my pastor, John, talked about whether or not faith can become an anecdote for burnout.[3] Toward the end of the interview, the host asked the three guests if they thought religious people felt loved when many other people felt unlovable. It was an interesting question, especially from a public radio host. I sensed a trace of both snarkiness and earnestness.

My pastor's response is something I've thought about several times since. John said that the system produces a shame-based culture. One that tells us, "you are nothing unless you can produce, unless you can measure up, unless your life matches your Instagram feed. And you cannot outrun that." But he goes on to add,

> The way I understand the message and the work of Jesus is that he's actually the one that's delivered me from that system and brought me into the kingdom of God, which is a kingdom for the poor, for the people that don't measure up, who aren't productive members of society. . . . The ones who knew they were worthless in the world's eyes, they were valued by him.[4]

That message, centered on innate human worth and not wage brackets or productivity, is refreshing and totally relevant. Our dignity in God is the opposite of a system of shame.

Imagine there were no culture wars, Christian nationalism, or Christian self-help. Just for a moment. In your mind, if you can remove the residue surrounding the church, do you see something verdant and lush growing? Something punk rock? It's small, but it's there. Can you feel it? When it is not distorted, the Christian story is radical, transformative, and convicting.

If Christianity is trustworthy—if Jesus really came to turn tables over and shift hearts outward, toward justice—then followers of Jesus can pray to have the courage to live like it is. As a cultural curiosity toward Christian practice grows, spiritual formation in community can nourish and offer a place of rest. Especially to those who are perpetually burned out, either from overwork or the anxiety of not having work.

I don't believe in work for work's sake, or that happiness alone is the end goal. Earning more, traveling fancier, and buying more possessions can turn us in on ourselves instead of unfolding our lives and opening them toward radical hospitality and shared community. Christians are offered a layered and rich "identity, transcendence, and community" in Jesus instead of in what we can accomplish in the market.

Gift Economy

Christians are part of Christ's capital-C church. We all get the same membership card to put on a keychain with our gym pass and library card. But American Christians also gain membership to another club, whether or not we want to belong: the market. The church and the market can't help but collide, often to spectacularly brutal consequences. If we're honest, the consumer in many of us can mutter at some base level that the church should do something for us as much as we should do something for the church.

Theologian Stephen Long writes about the difference between "gift" and "contract" in the 2007 book *Calculated Futures*. In an essay coauthored with Mennonite writer Tripp York, Long argues that the "competing practices" of the market and Christian practice depend on us orienting ourselves to the gift of liturgy rather than the contract of economic exchange. While we used to orient ourselves around cathedrals in Europe and Latin America positioned toward the east, "bearing witness to where Christian hope was directed—toward the homeland of Christ, who would one day return," we now orient ourselves around highways that lead to the mall. "The patterns and practices of our lives orient us in the world first and foremost as consumers."[5]

What we buy and how we spend our time tell us a lot about who we are—and how we want to be perceived. Our flash-in-the-pan obsessions are temporary liturgies that feel like first crushes. For a time I absolutely love Glossier boy brow, an eyebrow pencil that's been heavily marketed on my Instagram feed. I use it for a few months, but then I try the brow brush and color from another makeup company, Ilia, which advertises plant-based ingredients. I have little loyalty. Mom did, to Mr. Clean and unscented Dove soap.

In *Being Consumed*, Catholic theologian and ethicist William Cavanaugh argues that consumer culture commodifies everything. Yet, "most people are not overly attached to things, and most are not obsessed with hoarding riches . . . what really characterizes consumer culture is not attachment to things, but detachment."[6] The reason consumerism is a compelling frame for theology, Cavanaugh argues, is because it shapes our "spiritual disposition."[7] It is a posture. One that started for me in my Saturday morning cartoons childhood and stretches into my ship-lapped life today.

When I was a kid, I tried to gain some shred of popularity, or at least not lose my tepid social status, by the clothes I wore. Most of my friends did too. Some of us were more successful than others. In middle school, my husband shuffled to his locker with his backpack strategically covering the knock-off Guess jeans logo on his butt that had the triangle pointing up instead of down. In high school, identity for arty kids was superior if it was built on the found, rummaged, and repurposed. Lollapalooza '94 T-shirts, oversized maxi dresses, and itchy Pendleton pullover sweaters.

While there was a lite version of a popularity structure in high school, the possibilities for gaining social capital in my suburban church were nonexistent. Creative church kids intuitively looked for more depth, which led us to small pockets of Christian counterculture like Cornerstone. My friends and I wanted to find something unlikely, full of life and human emotion, and we wanted to look the part. To embody the interesting and infinite. We wanted night drives from youth group to an all-night diner with the windows down. Our own "spiritual disposition" was an attempt at an alternative marketplace—but was firmly rooted in consumer culture regardless.

Produce and Perform

In addition to work, modern American culture assigns self-worth to a second spoke of capitalism's wheel: lifestyle. An episode of the *Hidden Brain* podcast featuring public policy researcher Elizabeth Currid-Halkett explored cultural capital and consumerism. Currid-Halkett wrote about the "aspirational class" after observing how people today who identify as upper middle class, or affluent, less often show it. Instead of buying watches or silver spoons, she argues, one way class manifests itself today is through "healthy" choices like breastfeeding, doing yoga, and buying organic produce.[8]

Christianity's message is decidedly unaspirational. Jesus was born in the middle of nowhere to powerless people, a revolutionary teacher and outsider in a classist culture. Right now in Seattle and a lot of other places, the aspirational class is mostly white, definitely does yoga, and shops at the city's local co-op chain PCC. This is not a judgment that certain actions are wrong but an observation about what they imply culturally. Personally, I go to Barre class, shop at farmers' markets, and live on enough land to house a tiny orchard.

In my experience of living in the city, there's also a norm that the aspirational class does not attend church. Some of the reasons are practical and desirable. Maybe you work on Sunday. Or you've been working hard all week and want to stay in bed for an extra hour or two. But it's also cultural. Going to church does not fit into attending a Sunday brunch with a copy of the *New York Times* tucked under your arm.

What does the aspirational class look like in affluent American Christian culture? It might be how well versed we are in the enneagram, the size of our essential oil collection, how many meals on wheels we deliver, the number of likes we get on inspo posts, or any other banner we carry that inches higher than our truest identities as people of faith.

But the Christian story redefines our identities away from people who produce and purchase. Jesus untethers our worth from work and lifestyle and invites a loosening of our grip on the things we buy and the ways we fill our time.

The pandemic skewed productivity. Regular tasks like a trip to the grocery, now involving masks, multiple applications of hand sanitizer, and six-feet-apart lines, became Herculean errands. Many of us self-soothed during the pandemic in less than healthy ways. For me, that looked like sitting under several blankets on the porch, watching live performances of bands I like on YouTube, and eating mini peanut butter cups. Isn't the need for comfort as human as craving sugar, sex, or a pint of IPA after a long week?

Covid exhaustion reminds me of Petersen's *Buzzfeed* article. A lot of us were having trouble working, caregiving, and keeping a household going before the pandemic. Petersen writes, "when it came to the mundane, the medium priority, the stuff that wouldn't make my job easier or my work better, I avoided it."[9] Or, maybe it's more of a human and less of a Millennial attribute to avoid nagging tasks, one which is only heightened in a difficult season. Our parents called this a "honey-do list" (a gender-stereotyped phrase that may be worse than "adulting").

Jesus doesn't say that his followers will not be afflicted or get annoyed. He doesn't say there will be no spilled milk to sop up, income taxes to file late, toilets that overflow, or afternoons spent refreshing vaccine scheduling websites to find a slot for an aging parent. Instead, Christians are told to not let our hearts be troubled. The pandemic invited us to reorient our hearts not in spite of but in the very presence of daily disruptions layered on top of fear, uncertainty, and lack of control.

In these moments, I sometimes pray Psalm 18:19. "He brought me out into a spacious place; he rescued me because he delighted in me." The Christian story offers a spaciousness of the heart, a peace that isn't understandable and that holds steady with each daily trial, grief, and fear.

In pandemic life and regular life, we are not alone. Jesus offers release that is not contingent on ease but rather on his steadfast love. The countercultural and radical life of Jesus changes and challenges us, and the Holy Spirit resists being hemmed in by celebrity or brand.

Jesus Walks, Kanye Style

In the late 2010s, the media began reporting on a wave of celebrities who attended church. *Vox* was one of several outlets that covered Kanye West's "Sunday Service at the Mountain" at Coachella on Easter 2019. The event came with designer merch for sale in the "church clothes" tent, including sweatshirts a minimum wage–earning employee in California would have to work a couple of shifts to buy and $50 socks printed with the message "Jesus Walks."

"But church is incredibly cool right now," the article notes. "Particularly in California and among young celebrities—it's been used in recent years as a clean and easy rebranding strategy for famous people who get into hot water."[10] Such celeb-ification from this era offers evidence that, in certain settings, for some public people with enough cachet, it can be a surprise act of Hollywood rebellion to get churched.

Decades earlier, the spiritual geography of California and the American West had hosted Jesus People baptisms and Shirley Mac-

Laine's New Age workshops to find our "unlimited soul." The West Coast is a fertile landscape for trying new spirituality or coming back around to old-time religion—whether the draw is a celebrity, a personal vision quest, or any other unmet longing.

Regardless of geography, church is also experiential and well-suited for some Millennials with an inclination toward experiences. In 2019, a Harris Poll survey reported that 72 percent of Millennials will spend money on an experience rather than material possessions.[11]

Participants at Kanye's church at Coachella could both experience the spectacle and act as spectators. It was a show, for seeing and being seen. When I shop the fancy outdoor mall, I am being marketed to, typecast. I can buy clothes, accessories, cosmetics, tarot cards—and in each of these cases there is the chance to customize. I can choose the color of my iPhone (rose gold!), my favorite Glossier "cloud paint" blush color—and the depth I dip my toe into spiritual waters.

A Different System

The gospel delivers us from a system that tells us our self-worth is based on productivity and pay stubs. The people on the fringes were the very ones drawn to Jesus, and his message was at odds with capitalism. As Pope Francis told workers at an Italian steel manufacturer in 2017, "capitalism gives a moral cloak to inequality."[12]

Catholic social teaching talks specifically about the importance of Christian participation in social justice, including a preferential option for the poor, an idea coined by Gustavo Gutiérrez and championed by Salvadoran priest and activist Oscar Romero in the 1970s. Romero advocated for the rights of the oppressed and was assassinated. In the United States, Dorothy Day's Catholic Worker Movement began in the 1930s. Day's work embodied practical service, treating people with dignity while providing for basic needs.

However, while withdrawing from capitalism completely as a radical act of dependence on God is logically possible for some of us, doesn't that look a lot like opting out completely?

Christians are free to move in public spaces and work to make the world more equitable and just. But we're not all called to be desert ascetics or revolutionaries. We work to feed our families and make ends meet. We have responsibilities and limitations on our time and resources. Yet living differently, inspired by the saints who have come before us, is possible, even if the posture we can take is less radical.

Right where we are, right now, we can continue to practice simplicity and generosity of spirit. I think of St. Francis, who was born into plenty and walked away from it. He prayed,

> O divine Master, grant that I may not so much seek
> to be consoled as to console,
> to be understood as to understand,
> to be loved as to love.[13]

The brazen act of not expecting anything in return is truly un-aspirational—and so is to give more than we take.

CHAPTER 13

Burned but Not Consumed

You don't serve God by saying: "the Church is ineffective, I'll have none of it." Your pain at its lack of effectiveness is a sign of your nearness to God. We help overcome this lack of effectiveness simply by suffering on account of it. To expect too much is to have a sentimental view of life and this is a softness that ends in bitterness. Charity is hard and endures.

Flannery O'Connor

G od loves the sojourner. Deuteronomy 10:18 tells us that God "executes justice for the fatherless and the widow, and loves the sojourner" (ESV). In the biblical context, widows were members of a specific community to be treated with compassion. Sojourners were travelers who did not have a home—including people who fled unsafe situations and were living in Israel. This verse in the Pentateuch was talking about meeting practical, life and death needs. But it certainly still applies today, as those of us who have been formed by the American church bear grief and dismay at its moral failures and unholy allegiances.

Orphaned believers experience a sense of displacement, loss, and vulnerability like the biblical sojourner, forced into exile from our spiritual homes by the failings of the white evangelical church. We want to go to a safe place. And in God's hospitality, a new home can be built.

On Suffering

We can open our arms to affliction for any reason. But just one is good enough: to bear suffering on behalf of one another.

Where do those of us who wander rest? Where is our home when the church fails to make us welcome? Flannery O'Connor writes of the church that our "pain at its lack of effectiveness is a sign of [our] nearness to God. We help overcome this lack of effectiveness simply by suffering on account of it."[1]

All spiritually displaced people, lonely and grieving, are blessed and loved by God. You are known by God, seen plainly. Not one of us is lost or hidden. God is very near in the face of suffering.

In John 12:24, Jesus compares his followers to wheat. "Unless a grain of wheat falls into the earth and dies, it remains just a single grain; but if it dies it bears much fruit" (NRSVUE).

If American evangelicalism in its current iteration has been dying slowly, the politics and culture wars of the last few years have only accelerated our malignancies. Yeast to flour and water. But if Jesus is right in this verse—if the seed grain has to die to multiply and bear fruit—we can wait in full expectation for a new harvest. If O'Connor is right (and she usually is), for the church to bear fruit, we are called to suffer alongside it if we can.

Being called to suffer on behalf of a broken thing like the church can be incredibly uncomfortable. Yet, if our suffering in the name of the church moves us toward working to reform what is broken, we are indeed suffering for a reason. Our labor is not in vain.

All Things New

In Ezekiel 34, religious leaders in ancient Israel used power and prestige to their own gain. The similarities in these verses to predatory church leaders today is crystal clear. While called to be shepherds, the leaders are the very ones devouring their sheep. God has strong words of rebuke:

> As surely as I live, declares the Sovereign LORD, because my flock lacks a shepherd and so has been plundered and has become food for all the wild animals, and because my shepherds did not search for my flock but cared for themselves rather than for my flock, therefore, you shepherds, hear the word of the LORD: This is what the Sovereign LORD says: I am against the shepherds and will hold them accountable for my flock. I will remove them from tending the flock so that the shepherds can no longer feed themselves. I will rescue my flock from their mouths, and it will no longer be food for them. (vv. 8–10)

However, the passage continues on to build a picture of bright hope. The good shepherd, a foreshadowing of Christ, comes to the aid of the sheep. Finally, the land will be rid of the predators, and the yoke upon the necks of the flock will be broken.

> For this is what the Sovereign LORD says: I myself will search for my sheep and look after them. As a shepherd looks after his scattered flock when he is with them, so will I look after my sheep. I will rescue them from all the places where they were scattered on a day of clouds and darkness. (vv. 10–12)

Whether broken or on our way toward healing, we can call on Jesus to strengthen all beset by predatory leaders, be it ourselves or another person in our lives. Jesus sees the discouraged and devoured, and he is a God who is able to make all things new. In some sense, the church will always be broken because we, its members, are broken. But its healing continues with our own healing.

When we are ready, there is work we can do to reform the church, from condemning abuse to speaking out for denominational reform. There is also work we can do to heal ourselves if we have experienced spiritual trauma or abuse, including therapy and advocacy.

While we are in a healing place, it is OK to be quiet and inward. This is a season for gathering strength. We should take the time we need to receive good care. If Jesus is real, then the broken places are exactly where he will work in us through the Holy Spirit when we seek him and believe—Lord, help our unbelief.

Nothing Hidden

The work of personal and systemic restoration is the particular work of Jesus. It is the work he did on earth. Suffering with others—just as Christ did for us—is a radical act of empathy and a high calling. Finding trust to lean into this work is a base requirement that can, in and of itself, be hard to muster. Truly, we can only become a healing witness in the presence of our own suffering if we rise out of a safe place, empowered in our weakness by the Holy Spirit.

Throughout the Bible and recorded church history, there have been groups of people who have seen great loss, were almost overcome, and persevered. And in the end, a remnant of God's people remained steadfast and something new was born. That is why I am sure we still belong in the church.

We want a pure church. But there are endless ways for Christians to harm and fail ourselves and each other. When the church perpetuates harm, it's natural for us to want to disassociate ourselves from it for self-preservation, and sometimes it is wise to do so, for self-care.

But for some Christians, shying away from claiming our identity as a Christ follower contributes to a different sense of being orphaned. When we deny our identity to much of the watching world, we orphan ourselves.

Personally, I've found that opening up with friends about why I'm a Christian usually leads to curious and supportive conversations.

Somewhere along the way, I lost the burden of maintaining a double life and have been able to use the time I was spending on managing two identities in more constructive ways.

In all contexts, Christians can choose to be who we are. To say "I belong here" in humility, instead of taking a defensive, reactionary, or cloistered posture. To stand with hands low and palms open. To be plain. To not hide.

The Work of a Prophet

It is not a desirable thing to be a prophet. Prophets are in agony, because they want dearly for their generation to be whole and healthy but are rejected as they speak the words given them by God, including God's critique. No one wants to hear it. The prophet is alone.

Still, today, the church is called to be prophetic, even if a lot of people are shouting too loud to listen. The church is made up of people like you. If you're convicted of following Jesus, right now, in our very culture where much of Christianity has been Americanized, that conviction is prophetic hope. If that hope burns in your heart, pay attention to its heat.

When church reformers flourished in history, it was not with ease. They were following a prophetic call that strengthened them to press into God. Eventually this call led to a collective repentance that made straight the crooked places of many hearts.

Often, the tale is told that the early church was persecuted until, finally, the Roman Empire acknowledged Christianity in AD 323. But when elite Romans entered the church, many were not ethically formed or transformed by the way of Jesus. Instead, they persisted in their power machinations, politics, classism, and wealth accumulation—just Christianized by a veneer of baptism.

Some early Christians yearned for the purity of faith they'd practiced in persecution, before Christianity became the Roman Empire's official religion. Prior to those years, following Jesus required conviction because it came at a cost to safety and security. And so the monasteries of the desert mothers and fathers were formed.

There have been several reform movements within monasticism over the years that reacted to a disordered church. The desert mothers and fathers intentionally chose a life of difficulty, embracing asceticism. Cuban American theologian Justo L. Gonzalez wrote of the time these ascetics left the city for a nomadic existence:

> When the church joins the powers of the world, when luxury and ostentation take hold of Christian altars, when the whole of society is intent on turning the narrow path into a wide avenue, how is one to resist the enormous temptations of the times?[2]

These monks and hermits rejected a comfortable life for one spent pursuing holiness in the Egyptian desert. Some welcomed pilgrims from the city, while others formed desert communities.

There are many more examples. In the time of St. Francis, in the late 1100s and early 1200s, the church was an established, wealthy, and powerful institution. Francis centered on the needs of Christians and carried the true way of Jesus forward as a critique of the culture and church of the time.

In the early 1500s, the Protestant Reformation was a reaction to the power and excess of the church and was a response to clergy scandal and abuse. In the 1600s in Eastern Europe, the Moravian Brethren formed after fleeing the Bohemian Revolt and established a communal movement of Protestants motivated by simplicity and the teachings of Christ.

More recently, the Barmen Declaration of 1934 was a statement by European Christians, including Swiss theologian Karl Barth and Lutheran pastor Dietrich Bonhoeffer, which stood against the state church of Germany and religious institutions in the 1930s that accommodated the Nazis during the Holocaust. The sentiment from Article 3 in the statement rings true today: "We reject the false doctrine, as though the church were permitted to abandon the form of its message and order to its own pleasure or to changes in prevailing ideological and political convictions."[3]

Our present moment falls in a line after these and many more movements to reform and preserve the church from within. We are called to protect the church against corruption and welcome pluralism, not violence or insurrection to shield something that is broken and propagate power. A proper response to protecting the church is not to be surprised by brokenness but instead to grieve and to pray with fervor for renewal. To persistently love as a counterwitness against cultural forces.

What we need most are the voices of orphaned believers, people full of compassion who care for justice and truth. This is a position of value. If you are one of the voices calling the church to account, don't let the wolves push you out of your rightful place.

Birds of Prey

In the parable of the mustard seed, the smallest kernel becomes the biggest tree in the garden, so large that even eagles can nest there. The mustard tree grows broad enough to house birds of prey.

By now, we know to expect wolves with sheep. Vultures with sparrows. Our response is not to fly away from the tree but to chase off the vultures.

Birds of prey are weighing down the branches of modern evangelicalism. The vulture of whiteness has blinded the church to our racism. The beak of consumerism has stripped away the church's posture toward radical simplicity. The talons of sexism have suppressed the gifts of women and propagated the covering up of sexual abuse and a club of celebrity pastors. And the gathered wake of culture wars has severely damaged our credibility because, instead of spiritual formation, we have sought political posturing for power.

Has the American evangelical church irrevocably become synonymous with racism, nationalism, and Republicanism? Is the tree better lit on fire and burned to the stump? Because if evangelicalism is synonymous with white dominant culture, then there is little point trying to salvage it. If the tree is rotting, we're likely better off charting a new course.

Unless we can gather the courage to call the church toward repentance.

Why You Need the Church

Whatever the state of the church, we need it. I need it.

The church, the gathered body of believers, is a balm for the individualism and isolation bred into us by capitalism. Church is the relational core of the Christian life that can be both beautiful and stretching. I usually experience both of those feelings in a typical Sunday morning service at my church in Seattle.

Christianity requires us to be carried outside of ourselves—and beyond ourselves. To acknowledge there is a being who loves us and is completely other. A God who is outside of us and not in our control. That's how we transform.

Jesus took a band of friends with him during his three years of public ministry. They loved Jesus, and sometimes they quarreled with each other. One friend denied Jesus and another sold him out. The Christian life is often lived inside a community of people you wouldn't choose.

The early church understood the complexity of living life together in a charged time. To proclaim that Jesus, who had been publicly humiliated and executed, was Lord over Caesar was an audacious claim. They believed it with a conviction that carried them together across differences. We're called to bear the same message today.

The early church lived in the aftermath of their leader being condemned by the Romans and put to death, bonded in common purpose. Someone still had to make food and clean up after their meetings. We can take care of each other while we press against the powers that be.

There is a real risk in giving your time and emotions to a congregation that will inevitably, and probably repeatedly, cause you pain. Every long-term relationship opens us up to the certainty of hurt. But there can also be embodied grace in every hot casserole and prayer chain.

Because, unlike your neighbors or colleagues, you share the Holy Spirit with these awkward, mouthy, boring, intimidating, tender, funny, intuitive people. The ones with the gift of administration, or prayer, or discernment, or teaching. The people who keep you in check and remind you it's not about you, after all.

◆ ◆ ◆

These past few years have been like being in labor, and our choice has been to either brace for the next contraction or let the particular pain wash over us. When we stop resisting, the pain often doesn't leave or lessen. Instead, it becomes more defined and contained.

We need a community, small or large, to enter into the sacraments. The church is called to worship God, even when only two or three are gathered together. The communion elements are blessed and taken as we wait in line with other Christians, reaching back in time and looking ahead.

If we are looking for a church community but are isolated, finding a congregation may be incredibly difficult or feel impossible. If we can't find others who are safe and seeking Jesus, we can pray that God would bring the right people into our lives at the right time. We can pray just one word: "Help." I've had no other word to pray several times in the last few years, often in a place of desperation. And I've found that God often answers a prayer for help through other people.

Our worship with God and our relationships with other Christians are connected. The overlap is the church. Instead of being the place we must break away from to find liberation, the church is called to be the liberator. Entering and participating in any community means accepting limitations, and a church community is no different. The process of finding or choosing to stay in a church may involve letting go of the notion that a perfect body of believers exists.

Being a member of anything, especially the church, can be uncomfortable for many reasons, especially for those of us who have experienced trauma. Healthy, loving churches of broken people trying to follow Jesus do exist. It won't be hard to find faults even in healthy congregations. In fact, we'll be able to criticize them with ease.

Waiting for an ideal community will only bring no community. Committing to a church includes connecting to people as they actually are—not clinging to an idea of who we wish they were, or who we wish we could be. It can be difficult to feel comfortable, cool, and generally not awkward at church, especially for introverts. Let's face it, church life is awkward. It gets weird! But it is a place for our weird and awkward selves to be made welcome.

It is possible to be a part of the body of believers, because we're all stumbling together toward Jesus. Jesus loves us in our awkwardness. We are, together now, a broken community that needs each other's particular hang-ups, ideas, and quirks.

Why the Church Needs You

We need the church. And whatever the state of the American church, it needs us. Our relationship with the church is reciprocal.

The church can flourish again. In quiet corners, it has never ceased to flourish. Millions of Christians are worshiping around the world, especially in the Global South.

Christianity requires us to be carried outside of ourselves—and beyond ourselves. To acknowledge there is a being who loves us and is completely other. A God who is outside of us and not in our control.

The white evangelical church is rupturing for several reasons, including the industry of fear that was built around end times, culture wars that divided families and congregations with single-issue voting and nationalism, and a lack of spiritual formation that was no match to consumerism. The market has told us that instead of losing our life to find it, there is a way to self-actualize our best life and to keep spending until we find peace of mind and purpose.

The church is an institution—and any institution is really just a bunch of broken people. People aware of their brokenness are the most human. We are empathetic, in touch, and have eyes open to hypocrisy. We are the ones with the power to change things.

Those of us who have experienced and felt the failures of the church grieve deeply. Those of us who are without a home in this world but are very much invested in what happens here—with hearts that burn for change—are the very ones who can bear God's hope.

The church only needs one thing in order to revive, and it is totally out of human hands. The church requires the Spirit of God. The role of Christians in this work is clear: we are invited to heal from any pain we have experienced, repent for any wounds we have caused, and embody a better way forward. The three areas explored in this book—end times, culture wars, and consumerism—have worked together as catalysts behind the splintering of the white evangelical church, propagating racism and nationalism. But each can be reclaimed.

1. Instead of focusing on the end of the world, Christians are called to live redemptively in the present.

Premillennial dispensationalism centers on the apocalypse. It was a cultural marker of '60s and '70s evangelicalism. The rapture narrative was shared with many Boomers as a conversion strategy, as well as offering the comforting possibility of escape. Yet whether motivating or terrifying for our parents, it caused an undercurrent of fear to seep into the childhood of many evangelical Gen X and Millennial kids. As the years passed with no rapture, the apocalyptic idealism of some Boomer Christians turned to waiting, and waiting, and waiting for the next sign Jesus would finally return.

Some Christian dispensationalists persist in looking for the latest sign that the end is near, whether it's the next Mikhail Gorbachev forehead birthmark, the next Hillary, the next tsunami, or the next Arab Spring. Interestingly, Hal Lindsey himself wrote in *Late Great* to pay attention to signs of the times but still "plan our lives as though we will be here our full life expectancy."[4]

End-times culture creates an "us versus them" mentality: you're either in the boat and going to be rescued or bobbing in the water without a life preserver. This way of thinking hampers the true mission of the church, which is to be for the world, not apathetic to it.

Politicians like Ronald Reagan and conservative strategists leveraged evangelical fear of the apocalypse and single-issue voting to garner votes for the Republican Party. Today, there are traces of end-times fear woven into conspiracy theories and a generalized defensiveness against changing American demographics. The same fear of the world ending is felt in the nationalistic fear of the world changing.

We can hold fast against any pastor or politician who uses fear tactics to manipulate. Instead, we can vote with prayerful discernment for candidates who promote agency and dignity regardless of their party affiliation.

We're also called to value creation instead of waiting to escape from it. End-times culture tells us that the state of our planet is bad and is only going to get worse. The idea that believers will soon be raptured has created a church that doesn't adequately care for the environment or our communities. As we wait for Jesus to come again, each of us is a caregiver for the world. That responsibility was granted to Adam and Eve in the garden, and we carry it today.

Our neighbors' well-being has become less important than the security of our own lives. Instead, right teaching and discipleship include honoring our bodies while caring for the stranger and living with conviction that however eschatology unfolds, it is in Jesus's hands. We are tasked with being stewards of this world and each other. Living redemptively means being present in the here and now. We are to be for the world God has created and for each other—especially the countless people who have been left behind by structural powers that have magnified systemic racism.

We are called to care for the city and the country, to love people who believe like we do and those who are in tension with our beliefs—in other words, to support the well-being of people of all creeds and faiths, or else find we have supported none at all. We are called to be the hands and feet of Jesus in the world, not to preserve American exceptionalism to benefit Christian nationalism.

2. Instead of fighting culture wars, Christians are called to practice spiritual formation.

Most people, even those who do not identify as Christians, can sense the disingenuousness of pseudoreligiosity. When a celebrity or political candidate bends God to fit their brand, healthy spiritual formation helps us discern how the gospel message has been skewed or twisted.

Donald Trump was the front-runner for the Republican nominee for president when he spoke those infamous words in 2016 at Dordt University, a Christian school in Sioux Center, Iowa: "If I'm there, you're going to have plenty of power, you don't need anybody else," Trump told the crowd. "You're going to have somebody representing you very, very well. Remember that."[5]

In Romans 12:1, Paul writes, "Therefore, I urge you, brothers and sisters, in view of God's mercy, to offer your bodies as a living sacrifice, holy and pleasing to God—this is your true and proper worship." It's difficult to find a clearer counterexample to Paul's call to give our life to God as a posture of worship than the four words "Christianity will have power."

Instead of being a people in power, Christians are called to be a peculiar people who reject power to become, in Paul's words, living sacrifices. There's a sense in which followers of Jesus should be the most punk, never "selling out" to leaders who seek power at the cost of exclusion and harm. Resisting engagement in culture wars helps us to keep clear focus on our calling. When Jesus was alive, his followers were undefined by any dominant group, be it Pharisees, Sadducees, zealots, or Romans. We can regain that sense of counterculture. We can be a people who are outwardly focused, drawing people in instead of building walls and hunkering down behind them.

Instead of a framework of power, the way of following Jesus includes a distinctive and counterintuitive ethic. An ethic that focuses on building character, having compassion and integrity, and making hard choices even when doing so leads to loss. We are called to live out what we believe. As James says, "Show me your faith without deeds, and I will show you my faith by my deeds" (James 2:18).

An ethical framework where Christians essentially "show our work" in serving the world may sound dangerously works-based instead of grace-based to some Protestants. But our beliefs are made manifest by works. They are a matter of faith. If I do not act in tandem with what I profess to believe, I show myself to essentially be an atheist, even if I speak fluent Christianese.

How we live matters, and Christians are called to live differently. That is why when faith is infused throughout our lives, our lives naturally include works.

Liturgy, the work of the people, is for everyone. Nationalists need formation. Cultural Christians need formation. Christians who remain in the church but are left in the wake of politics and culture wars need formation. Formation is an equalizer, a path to unification, for we all have dark hearts clouded by our own geography, social status, and political views.

Our life liturgy, the spiritual practices we adopt, result in our formation. We are formed by what we ingest. If I wake up, dress for the weather, go for a walk, and pray, my morning is set on a different course than if I grab the phone off my bedside table after my alarm rings and check the news. The places I choose to spend my free time and the content I read, watch, and listen to impact my worldview and the state of affairs in my spirit.

To be sure our routines are aligned with our values, we can try to wait a little longer before acting and pray on our own and alongside others. We can apply ideas like Jesuit indifference and Quaker clearness committees into any discernment. "When we talk about spiritual formation we are talking about framing a progression of life in which people come to actually do all things that Jesus taught," Dallas Willard writes. "So we are obviously going for the heart. We are aiming for a change of the inner person, where what we do originates."[6]

There is no disembodied faith. Healthy formation, doing "all the things Jesus taught," changes our inner selves and sets us free to serve. Formation sets our gaze on an arc of dignity instead of an arc of power. Rooted in personal and corporate disciplines, the Christian life becomes a way of being that challenges dominant culture instead of being formed by it. That is our right call and ethic.

3. Instead of being defined by producing and purchasing, we can cultivate a posture of generosity.

Capitalism works to form us. The internet, economics, careers, politics, and cultural trends inform how we see the world. Evangelicalism never significantly differentiated itself as a clear path away from the stadium, food court, or strip mall. But the American church can no longer cede the ground of formation to consumer culture. Faith does not work like consumerism does.

Marketing sells us an illusion: that everything can be customized to meet, match, and multiply our interior desires. There is no limitation to the optimized life we are told we can create. If a product does not work, a customer can be assured of a full refund. Faith, in contrast, is not a transaction. It is a far riskier proposition.

We are limited, fallible, and fragile. Eventually, our exercise in free choice will fail. Consumerism creates winners and losers, but the gospel offers a counternarrative to America's radical individualism. When Jesus was asked to identify the most important law, he said to love God with our whole selves and love our neighbors as ourselves. Love of neighbor moves us toward a posture of generosity. God's abundant love does not run out or wear out, and it cannot be bought and sold. There is always enough for one more. Without community, our positive-vibes-best-life-ever will crumble, because it is not flesh and blood real.

We are all made equally in God's image. The *imago Dei* gives each person full dignity and value. But consumerism values people with celebrity and influence more than those of us who are differently abled in body or mind. Even those of us who pass as beautiful and successful can end up jockeying so hard that we become burned out, neglecting our souls for the sake of social position.

Those of us who do not qualify as young enough, thin enough, or financially secure enough are the people Jesus longs for. The displaced, oppressed, excluded, unpopular, poor, and afflicted are the very ones the church should be serving with full welcome and giving a place of honor.

Instead of following influencers, we can allow Jesus to spark our spiritual imagination to reevaluate work, self-image, and the way we buy. Downsizing rather than upsizing our lives is countercultural, because the world says we should take more on, clock in more hours, and exchange what is worn out for what is new. We don't have to follow that path. We can prioritize relationships and healthy care for ourselves and each other rather than trying to access or maintain membership in the aspirational class.

Why I'm Still a Christian

In the synagogue in Capernaum, Jesus told his followers, "I am the bread of life . . . the living bread that came down from heaven. Whoever eats this bread will live forever. This bread is my flesh, which I will give for the life of the world" (John 6:48, 51). This bread does not fill the stomach for a little while but instead fortifies the soul. At hearing this teaching, many disciples began to turn away from Jesus. It was too much. They could not exchange the currency of belief for the risk of rejection that came from identifying as a follower of Jesus.

Consider these people with tenderness, because they were close to complete surrender, heartbreakingly close.

I wonder what happened to those who left. Would that day in Capernaum calcify into a memory that held the faint possibility of an electric turn? Or would some slight wind later in life rotate their mind back to the moment they almost followed? The offer of redemption does not expire.

These words Jesus said about bread were spoken close to the end of his life. Jesus knew what would happen next. But before Judas betrayed him and bought the barren field, "many of his disciples turned back and no longer followed him" (v. 66).

Jesus understands the feeling of irrelevance that comes from staying while others go. From downsizing while others hoard. From feeling the sting of being labeled foolish and the bitter quiet of being abandoned.

> "You do not want to leave too, do you?" Jesus asked the Twelve.
>
> Simon Peter answered him, "Lord, to whom shall we go? You have the words of eternal life." (vv. 67–68)

I am a Christian because there is nowhere else for me to go. I am a Christian because of the still, small voice. Ironically, at points I am a Christian because I am sure of the existence of evil—and that evil is evidence for a counterpart of blinding goodness. I am a Christian because, for me, the end of the world has become less about an apocalypse and more about a joining of the human heart with the sacred, burning heart of Jesus.

I am here because I want to sit at the feast in the end, with the good wine and hearty bread. Because I can see part of the Olympic mountains from my bathtub, and I believe in the divine creation, from base to summit. Sometimes I am a Christian because someone else needs me to believe on their behalf for a little while.

I am a Christian because, even though I am made to wander, I walked for miles until there was no trail left. My spirit felt at rest in a meeting of the Holy Spirit. Simply, I am a Christian because of God's free, infinite love.

No Spotless Lambs

There are no spotless lambs in this room. Our bodies become sick or are imperfect. No one would qualify to be a sacrifice in the temple. Human thoughts are clouded; we are not pure.

In Deuteronomy 15:21, we're told of sacrificial lambs that "If an animal has a defect, is lame or blind, or has any serious flaw, you must not sacrifice it to the LORD your God." But because Jesus offered his perfect body, our flawed bodies, hungry hearts, and distracted minds are not disqualified. It is so tender and lovely that our stories are placed onto the altar. That without shame we can move closer to Christ's perfect body. To become more holy as an act of "true and proper worship" (Rom. 12:1).

Even now we can change. Compared to the glow of Christ, politics and culture wars are dim lights in a foggy field. The clear light of Christ is everything. Like St. Patrick said, there is Christ before, behind, below, and above.

The timeless, omnipotent Spirit of God wants to dwell in our bodies, which do and think stupid things. Which grow people and lose people. Which mourn and grieve and eat processed food and go to the movies. Which get old and slow. Which age and produce cysts, which divide cells and kill us from within. The Holy Spirit wants to dwell in our deterioration. Because the Holy Spirit is that good.

To live the Christian life, we can choose to accept the possibility that God is not just real but loving. God's love follows us. It doesn't stay in one place. As Psalm 23 teaches us, whenever there is a valley, there is a staff to steady and a rod to protect. Whenever there is a wilderness, there is a table. Whenever there is wine, it overflows the cup and revives.

There is a feast at the end of the story, and it is abundant.

Burned but Not Consumed

The symbol of the Irish Presbyterian church is a burning bush with the Latin phrase *ardens sed virens*: "burning but flourishing."[7] We are burned but not consumed.

It starts with the tiny flame of personal transformation, an orphan coming home. Then the tiny flame gathers fuel for the work ahead, reforming the American church from the inside out.

At Pentecost, believers experienced "what seemed to be tongues of fire that separated and came to rest on each of them" (Acts 2:3), and that same Spirit burns in Christian hearts today. When we bear the weight of doubt that is at times crushing—a cloud moving overhead, bringing daily desolations—we burn but are not consumed. Nothing God sees is wasted. Channel your pain and suffering into compassion. The continuation of the church needs orphaned believers to lead as the desert fathers and mothers, Anabaptists, and many other reformers throughout church history led.

When people we love leave the church—or we leave a church in fresh grief—we burn but are not consumed. Instead, we wait in full expectation that all will be made well.

That idea—that we will experience full and complete restoration—is part of the revealed Christian tradition and a place of shared faith among believers past and present. To dare to live in this kind of expectation is exceedingly difficult. Some of us or our loved ones are at this moment unhealed and hold lasting trauma; some have sick bodies or are overwhelmed by addiction or mental illness.

As I write this, the initial Christian unity denouncing the murder of George Floyd has been usurped by rhetoric around Critical Race Theory in many parts of America. The Covid pandemic has burned out pastors and left congregants wondering how their home congregations can be so vastly divided on issues affecting the common good, like masks.

Tent encampments are found near many off- and on-ramps around Seattle and other cities, a reminder of the unsolved homelessness crisis and lack of a social safety net.

There are too many more places of pain to list. Opioids and methamphetamine. Sexual assault and cover-ups.

As I write, the Ukrainian city of Kharkiv is being bombed and Kyiv is surrounded by a multitude of Russian armed forces, a fresh reminder that war should not exist. But it does, and it is vicious.

In the presence of these enemies and many more, the biblical story holds that all will, satisfyingly and completely, be set right. This hope is what hearts yearn for. We cry out for justice in our spirits. Because any version of Christianity that doesn't include the reality of all being made well is an insubstantial myth.

Today we can choose to live in light of the great hope of an even greater welcoming of orphans to come. A new homecoming. A better country (Heb. 11:16)—a heavenly one. And until that time, we can move closer to our own healing and the healing of Christ's church.

This moment, in each Christian, the tiny flame burns day and night. No affliction can overcome the Spirit of God in us. The whole neon, buzzing, wild world of the Holy Spirit is hovering and healing. Being loud and being quiet.

Here is where we want to be. Here is where we are whole.

It doesn't matter if the church is reformed quickly or slowly. If our hearts are hungry or receiving complete nutrition. All that matters is Christ. Loyal, thick, bioluminescent, eternal love. Love kindled in our grotesque and gorgeous minds, bodies, souls, and spirits. Love that is burned but not consumed.

EPILOGUE

What does God say about being orphaned? In Psalm 68:5, we're told "Father of the fatherless and protector of widows is God in his holy habitation" (ESV).

I am not fatherless.

This winter, as I finish this book, I have a father. He has cancer in his bones, but it is well managed, and he is in remission. Right now, my father is alive, and my mother is alive, and they live ten minutes from my house. We could reach them with almost no delay.

Tonight, Dad sits on the couch waiting to be raptured and is also thinking about errands he has to run this week. He lost his taste buds from chemo, but he kept a sweet tooth. There are wintergreen Lifesavers in his pocket. When you bite into a wintergreen Lifesaver in the dark, electrons and nitrogen molecules bump up against each other. There is the smell of mint and a flash of light.

If my father dies in the middle of the night, I imagine the moment his soul leaves his body. Will there be a spark?

Tonight, my living father sits in sweatpants and a T-shirt from his collection of Jewish-Christian tropes: "Everybody Loves a Jewish Boy." "Shofar, So-Good!" "Don't Worry, Be Jewish." "Oy Vey!" And the T-shirt he's had since I was a kid, which I used to sleep in: "I Survived a Jewish Mother."

He bought that one in New York City in the '80s from a vendor near Times Square. It is red with white letters. Dad survived his Jewish mother, and I will survive my Jewish father. I will live longer than my father, and I will die like my father will die. And if there is a literal rapture in between, then thanks be to God.

Dad knows that I am writing this book, and that he is a central character. I want him to read every word in it. I have read parts of the manuscript to him along the way, and I hope he is able to read the whole thing before he dies. But he told me he doesn't feel the need to read this book with any sense of urgency. When he imagines not being here to see the complete, published book, he thinks of it joyfully. Because that could only mean he was raptured. He would be too happy then to miss the book. Having seen or not seen what I wrote about him wouldn't matter.

Dad says he doesn't care if I buy a funeral plot and has no opinion about what we'll put on his gravestone. He says planning for a funeral is a waste of money.

I've asked Dad on a few occasions during his illness where he would like to be buried, and he always says the same thing: "Put me in a pine box."

In my mind, his dead body is under the ground in a blue suit. But instead of burial herbs and spices, he is embalmed with sugar and color.

My father's body was never a temple. He always moves at a certain clip. Takes extra helpings. Keeps drawers full of original ChapStick, mini Kleenexes, Chiclets, and cheap sunglasses. There are empty plastic water bottles everywhere in the back of the car. Still, he is never replenished or revived. Like a lot of us, he has taken more than he has given.

His pace is fast, and his beliefs are supersized with speculation, but there is a tenderness to my father's spirit. Even sick, he would do anything to help. The dry cleaner, the post office, school pickup.

Dad has always been vexed by fame. At the end of his life, he is still waiting to be famous. He knows that is not Christlike, but he cannot help it. Tom Weinraub wants the world to know he was here. He had a life, and it was big-small. He was a light switch to people—he was on for you or off for you. But if he was on, he was an illumination.

If Dad is wrong, and he is not raptured. If his body is in the pine box. If he never gets to be lifted to heaven in his lifetime. Still, he wants to be remembered. It's the least we could do.

Can someone truly believe they will be raptured? Can a rational, functional person believe they will literally and totally be lifted from their living room into heaven?

My father will believe until the end. If we could only believe half as much about something good and true as my father believes in the rapture. If only our hearts could burn for that long. But "My God," will they say, "Tom was one of a kind." "My God, did he believe in Jesus the whole way through."

"My God," I will tell them, "did he love me, and wreck me, and love me back."

ACKNOWLEDGMENTS

Thank you to the friends who read chapters of this book early, with clear feedback and encouragement: Strahan Coleman, Leonetta Elaiho, Josh Jeter, Dan Koch, and Temitope Peters.

Thanks to the Bindery Agency, my agent John Blase, and the "First Five" who began to work with John in 2021: Tommy Brown, Seth Haines, Sara McDaniel, and Lore Ferguson Wilbert. We're the lucky ones.

John, you'll be proud to learn that at your prompting I taped an index card to the wall above my desk with the two words Anthony Hopkins grunts out in Jim Harrison's *Legends of the Fall* to brace for critics of my work, starting with myself: Screw 'em.

Thanks to Winn Collier, Marilyn McEntyre, and my peers in the sacred art of writing DMin program at the Eugene Peterson Center for the Christian Imagination at Western Theological Seminary. While the suggestion that Baker create a watermark in the shape of Mikhail Gorbachev's birthmark to use as a section divider in this book did not make it past the design department, I knew then that you would bring collective humor, warmth, and levity to this work.

Thanks to Baker Books, particularly Stephanie Duncan Smith, for your cool sensibility, uncommonly sharp editorial eye, and risk-taking on a first-time author who leans floaty. And thanks to the Baker editorial and marketing team who supported this book: Erin Bartels, Hannah Boers, Melanie Burkhardt, Eileen Hanson, Carson Kunnen, Laura Palma, Olivia Peitsch, and Robin Turici.

Thanks to Patti Smith and Michael Stipe for introducing me to the kind of writing that strings together nouns when I was in high school, and basically for forming my aesthetic. You'll probably never read this, but you helped make it possible.

Thanks to Linford Detweiler and Karin Bergquist of the band Over the Rhine, particularly for your song "All My Favorite People," which introduced me to two words that have defined my own experience in the world, along with that of many others: *orphaned believer*. Your music has been a constant companion over the last twenty-five years.

To the folks at Grace for praying alongside me for the past four years, since this book was an idea. Thank you.

To Michelle. Thank you for Hudson and the mountain medicine.

To Mom, thank you for giving Dad the spotlight because you knew he needed it.

Dad, I told you once that you're my best friend, and I meant it.

Asher and Sabine, you bring joy and you bring life, and you're both the best thing I'll ever create.

Drew, I heard a line on a television show about a couple being married for so long they have become a new, four-legged creature. It is a weird image, and it's perfect. After multiple decades, we are our own animal. This book, at its heart, is an outline of our shared work as we move through this wild world together.

NOTES

Introduction

1. Pew Research Center, "Report: America's Changing Religious Landscape," Pew Research Center Religious Demographics, May 12, 2015, https://www.pewforum .org/2015/05/12/americas-changing-religious-landscape/.

2. Pew Research Center, "The Unaffiliated Who Are in the Seattle Metro Area," *Religious Landscape Study*, accessed May 19, 2022, https://www.pewforum.org/rel igious-landscape-study/metro-area/seattle-metro-area/religious-tradition/unaffil iated-religious-nones/.

3. Stephen Asma, "Op-Ed: Religiously Unaffiliated 'Nones' Are Pursuing Spirituality, but Not Community," *Los Angeles Times*, June 7, 2018, https://www.latimes .com/opinion/op-ed/la-oe-asma-nones-spirituality-20180607-story.html.

Chapter 1 Risky Business

1. Michael Graham and Skyler Flowers, "The Six Way Fracturing of Evangelicalism," June 7, 2021, https://mereorthodoxy.com/six-way-fracturing-evangelicalism/.

2. Harvey Sullivan, "'End of Days' Bible Prophecy Fulfilled after Birth of Red Heifer in Israel," September 10, 2018, https://www.thesun.co.uk/news/7217719/bible -prophecy-apocalypse-firs-red-heifer-born-israel/.

3. Anne Helen Petersen and Kristin Kobes Du Mez, "*Jesus and John Wayne* and Mel Gibson's William Wallace from the Movie *Braveheart*," *Culture Study*, September 22, 2021, https://annehelen.substack.com/p/jesus-and-john-wayne?s=r.

4. "A Quote by Mother Teresa," Goodreads, accessed June 28, 2022, https://www .goodreads.com/quotes/6946-not-all-of-us-can-do-great-things-but-we.

Chapter 2 Sad Confetti

1. Erica Beringer, "Dozens of Headstones Vandalized at Fort Wayne Jewish Cemetery," WISHTV, February 3, 2016, https://www.wishtv.com/news/dozens-of -headstones-vandalized-at-fort-wayne-jewish-cemetery/.

2. Hal Lindsey with Carole C. Carlson, *The Late Great Planet Earth* (Grand Rapids: Zondervan, 1970).

3. Erin A. Smith et al., "*The Late Great Planet Earth* Made the Apocalypse a Popular Concern," *Humanities* 38, no. 1 (Winter 2017), https://www.neh.gov/hum anities/2017/winter/feature/the-late-great-planet-earth-made-the-apocalypse-pop ular-concern.

4. Janet Maslin, "Film: A 'Planet' Doomed," *New York Times*, January 18, 1979, https://www.nytimes.com/1979/01/18/archives/film-a-planet-doomed.html.

5. Marjorie Hyer, "Armageddon," *The Washington Post*, October 24, 1984, https://www.washingtonpost.com/archive/politics/1984/10/24/armageddon/8b364a1c-fadc-41e1-b2d1-b262aa08eb46/.

6. WebMD Editorial, "Spiritual Abuse: How to Identify It and Find Help," WebMD, accessed March 6, 2022, https://www.webmd.com/mental-health/signs-spiritual-abuse.

Chapter 3 End-Times Kids

1. Michael McVicar, *Christian Reconstruction* (Chapel Hill, NC: University of North Carolina Press, 2015), 140.

2. Timothy Weber, "Dispensational Premillennialism: The Dispensationalist Era," *Christian History*, January 1, 1999, https://www.christianitytoday.com/hist ory/issues/issue-61/dispensational-premillennialism-dispensationalist-era.html.

3. Matthew Avery Sutton, *American Apocalypse: A History of Modern Evangelicalism* (Cambridge, MA: Belknap Press, 2017), 18.

4. Rund Abdelfatah and Ramtin Arablouei, "Apocalypse Now," *Throughline*, June 13, 2019, https://www.npr.org/transcripts/731664197.

5. Michael J. Vlach, "Dispensational Theology," The Gospel Coalition, accessed March 6, 2022, https://www.thegospelcoalition.org/essay/dispensational-theology/.

6. Abdelfatah and Arablouei, "Apocalypse Now."

7. Weber, "Dispensational Premillennialism."

8. Abdelfatah and Arablouei, "Apocalypse Now."

9. Erin A. Smith et al., "*Late Great Planet Earth.*"

10. McVicar, *Christian Reconstruction*, 140.

11. Erin A. Smith et al., "*Late Great Planet Earth.*"

12. Erin A. Smith et al., "*Late Great Planet Earth.*"

13. Erin A. Smith et al., "*Late Great Planet Earth.*"

14. Rory Carroll, "America's Dark and Not-Very-Distant History of Hating Catholics," *Guardian*, September 12, 2015, https://www.theguardian.com/world /2015/sep/12/america-history-of-hating-catholics.

15. Art Levine, "The Devil in Gorbachev," *The Washington Post*, June 5, 1988, https://www.washingtonpost.com/archive/opinions/1988/06/05/the-devil-in-gor bachev/34f9db9b-9498-4894-9800-90f7d3d4e434/.

16. "A Distant Thunder (a Thief in the Night Part 2)," YouTube video, 1:16:37, uploaded by Christian Movies, May 1, 2020, https://www.youtube.com/watch?v=7jVU0m73iQk.

17. Pew Research Center, "Section 3: War, Terrorism and Global Trends," *Report: Public Sees a Future Full of Promise and Peril*, June 22, 2010, https://www .pewresearch.org/politics/2010/06/22/section-3-war-terrorism-and-global-trends/.

18. "Address during the Cuban Missile Crisis," JFK Library, accessed March 7, 2022, https://www.jfklibrary.org/learn/about-jfk/historic-speeches/address-during-the-cuban-missile-crisis.

19. "A Look Back at America's Fallout Shelter Fatuation," CBS News, October 7, 2010, https://www.cbsnews.com/news/a-look-back-at-americas-fallout-shelter-fatuation/.

20. Sarah Pruitt, "At Cold War Nuclear Fallout Shelters, These Foods Were Stocked for Survival," History, February 26, 2020, https://www.history.com/news/cold-war-fallout-shelter-survival-rations-food.

21. Charles King and Gods of the Upper Air, "White Evangelicals Must Choose Reform or Extremism," *Time*, March 1, 2021, https://time.com/5942445/reform-evangelical-christianity/.

22. Derek S. Hicks, "Eschatology in African American Theology," Oxford Handbooks Online, August 1, 2014, https://www.oxfordhandbooks.com/view/10.1093/oxfordhb/9780199755653.001.0001/oxfordhb-9780199755653-e-017.

23. From a speech given by Martin Luther King Jr. on April 3, 1968 at Mason Temple in Memphis, Tennessee. "Martin Luther King, Jr. I've Been to the Mountaintop," americanrhetoric.com, https://www.americanrhetoric.com/speeches/mlk ivebeentothemountaintop.htm.

24. Tara Isabella Burton, "#Raptureanxiety Calls out Evangelicals' Toxic Obsession with the End Times," *Vox*, December 13, 2017, https://www.vox.com/2017/12/12/16763230/raptureanxiety-calls-out-evangelicals-obsession-with-the-end-times-roy-moore-evangelical-jerusalem.

25. Dan Koch, "End Times Anxiety: Part 1 (#50)," January 13, 2020, in *You Have Permission*, podcast, Apple Podcasts, https://podcasts.apple.com/us/podcast/end-times-anxiety-part-1-50/id1448000113?i=1000462348895.

26. Erin A. Smith et al., *"Late Great Planet Earth."*

27. *Apocalyptic Literature* (podcast), "Apocalypse Please," episode 1, BibleProject Podcast, April 27, 2020, https://bibleproject.com/podcast/apocalypse-please/.

Chapter 4 One Way

1. Joan Didion, "Slouching towards Bethlehem," *Saturday Evening Post*, repr. June 14, 2017, https://www.saturdayeveningpost.com/2017/06/didion/. Originally published on September 23, 1967.

2. Carol McGraw, "Flashback," *The Washington Post*, July 19, 1997, https://www.washingtonpost.com/archive/local/1997/07/19/flashback/7acb2986-9d8f-4576-9cc9-e44fda613e42/.

3. Larry Eskridge, *God's Forever Family: The Jesus People Movement in America* (New York: Oxford University Press, 2013), 86.

4. "The Armageddon Experience—One Way (Live Explo 72 / 1972)," YouTube video, 3:39, uploaded by Classic Christian Rock, June 17, 2020, https://www.youtube.com/watch?v=0MoYtlhdirw.

5. Patrick Metzger, "The Nostalgia Pendulum: A Rolling 30-Year Cycle of Pop Culture Trends," *The Patterning* (blog), February 13, 2017, https://thepatterning.com/2017/02/13/the-nostalgia-pendulum-a-rolling-30-year-cycle-of-pop-culture-trends/.

6. "The Cornerstone Festival: Twenty Years and Counting (2003)," YouTube video, 1:24:00, uploaded by coffinbuilder, August 11, 2013, https://www.youtube .com/watch?v=XSetI87n8SM.

7. "The Cornerstone Festival."

8. "The Cornerstone Festival."

9. Neil J. Young, "The Summer of Love Ended 50 Years Ago. It Reshaped American Conservatism," *Vox*, August 31, 2017, https://www.vox.com/the-big -idea/2017/8/31/16229320/summer-of-love-jesus-people-religious-right-history.

10. Young, "Summer of Love Ended 50 Years Ago."

11. "Larry Norman & His Son Mike; It's Complicated . . ." Audible.com, October 26, 2020, https://www.audible.com/pd/Larry-Norman-his-son-Mike-Its-Complic ated-Podcast/B08KYZ1MP5.

12. Christopher Smith, "JPUSA: A Tragic History of Sexual Abuse," *Slow Church* (blog), March 1, 2014, https://www.patheos.com/blogs/slowchurch/2014/03/01 /jpusa-a-tragic-history-of-sexual-abuse/.

13. Eskridge, *God's Forever Family*, 263.

14. Wikipedia, s.v. "Jews for Jesus," accessed March 6, 2022, https://en.wikipedia .org/wiki/Jews_for_Jesus.

15. Michael Luo, "Jews for Jesus Hit Town and Find a Tough Crowd," *New York Times*, July 4, 2006, https://www.nytimes.com/2006/07/04/nyregion/04push.html.

16. Jonathan Romain, "Did Moishe Rosen Die a Jew or a Christian?" *Guardian*, June 23, 2010, https://www.theguardian.com/commentisfree/belief /2010/jun/23/moishe-rosen-jew-jesus.

17. Barna Group, "Almost Half of Practicing Christian Millennials Say Evange- lism Is Wrong," Barna Group, February 5, 2019, https://www.barna.com/research /millennials-oppose-evangelism/.

Chapter 5 Old Fear, New Age

1. Eskridge, *God's Forever Family*, 296.

2. Chris Moody, "The Millennials Arrive at America's Most Famous Hippie Community," *New Republic*, July 9, 2019, https://newrepublic.com/article/154123 /millennials-arrive-americas-famous-hippie-community.

3. Steven Brocklehurst, "Children of God Cult Was 'Hell on Earth,'" BBC News, June 27, 2018, https://www.bbc.com/news/uk-scotland-44613932.

4. Stephanie Buck, "The Hippie Christian Cult That Encouraged Sex with Chil- dren Is Still around Today," Timeline, January 17, 2017, https://timeline.com/child ren-of-god-5245a45f6a2a?gi=16a1df0b2341.

5. J. Gordon Melton, ed., "The Way International," accessed March 7, 2022, https://www.britannica.com/topic/The-Way-International.

6. James R. Lewis, "15," in *Magical Religion and Modern Witchcraft* (Albany: State University of New York Press, 1996), 344.

7. Nina Easton, "Shirley MacLaine's Mysticism for the Masses : She's the Super Saleswoman for a Fast-Growing New Age Movement," *Los Angeles Times*, September 6, 1987, https://www.latimes.com/archives/la-xpm-1987-09-06-tm-6352-story.html.

8. Douglas Coupland, *Generation X: Tales for an Accelerated Culture* (New York: St. Martin's Press, 1991), 166.

9. Bruce Buursma, "TV Religion Ratings Are Sky-High," *Chicago Tribune*, October 26, 1985, https://www.chicagotribune.com/news/ct-xpm-1985-10-26-8503130362 -story.html.

10. Margaret Talbot, "A Mighty Fortress," *New York Times*, February 27, 2000, https://www.nytimes.com/2000/02/27/magazine/a-mighty-fortress.html.

11. Talbot, "A Mighty Fortress."

12. Miroslav Volf, "Floating Along?" *The Gospel and Our Culture* 12, no. 1 (March 2000), https://gocn.org/wp-content/uploads/2015/11/121-newsletter_0_0.pdf.

13. Walter Brueggemann, *The Prophetic Imagination* (Minneapolis: Fortress Press, 2018), 45.

14. Mark A. Noll, *The Scandal of the Evangelical Mind* (Grand Rapids: Eerdmans, 1995).

Chapter 6 Hot Buttons

1. Content from this chapter was taken from the author's article: "There Are Evangelicals Who Stand Against Trump. I'm One of Them," *New York Times*, November 1, 2020, https://www.nytimes.com/2020/11/01/opinion/trump-evangelicals .html.

2. David French, "Donald Trump's Strength Might also Be His Fatal Political Weakness," *Atlantic*, December 16, 2021, https://newsletters.theatlantic.com/the -third-rail/61bb740005e48f0021110e64/donald-trumps-strength-might-also-be-his -fatal-political-weakness/.

3. Quoted in Yonat Shimron, "Study: Most White Evangelicals Don't Want to Live in a Religiously Diverse Country," *Religion News Service*, November 11, 2021, https://religionnews.com/2021/11/01/study-most-white-evangelicals-dont-want-to -live-in-a-religiously-diverse-country/.

4. Matthew Avery Sutton, "The Capitol Riot Revealed the Darkest Nightmares of White Evangelical America," *New Republic*, January 14, 2021, https://newrepublic .com/article/160922/capitol-riot-revealed-darkest-nightmares-white-evangelical -america.

5. Alan Shlemon, "Are the Unborn a Convenient Group to Advocate For?," Stand to Reason, October 12, 2021, https://www.str.org/w/are-the-unborn-a-convenient -group-to-advocate-for-.

6. Neil O'Brian, "Evangelicals Opposed Abortion Long before Their Leaders Caught Up," *The Washington Post*, May 17, 2022, https://www.washingtonpost.com /politics/2022/05/18/dodds-evangelicals-roe-conservative-opinion/.

7. Randall Balmer, "The Real Origins of the Religious Right," *Politico*, May 27, 2014, https://www.politico.com/magazine/story/2014/05/religious-right-real-ori gins-107133/.

8. Stephen Hess, "Jimmy Carter: Why He Failed," Brookings, January 21, 2000, https://www.brookings.edu/opinions/jimmy-carter-why-he-failed/.

9. Randall, "Real Origins of the Religious Right."

10. Evangelical Press, "Bob Jones University Drops Interracial Dating Ban," *Christianity Today*, March 1, 2000, https://www.christianitytoday.com/ct/2000/marchweb -only/53.0.html.

11. "Miscegenation Laws," Tennessee Secretary of State, accessed May 9, 2022, https://sharetngov.tnsosfiles.com/tsla/exhibits/blackhistory/pdfs/Miscegenation%20laws.pdf.

12. Katelyn Beaty, "Bob Jones U. Apologizes for Former Racist Policies," *Christianity Today*, November 21, 2008, https://www.christianitytoday.com/news/2008/november/bob-jones-u-apologizes-for-former-racist-policies.html.

13. Balmer, "Real Origins of the Religious Right."

14. Gillian Frank and Neil J. Young, "What Everyone Gets Wrong about Evangelicals and Abortion," *The Washington Post*, May 16, 2022, https://www.washingtonpost.com/outlook/2022/05/16/what-everyone-gets-wrong-about-evangelicals-abortion/.

15. Holly Lebowitz Rossi, "Historian Calls for an Evangelical Reckoning on Race," *Publishers Weekly*, August 9, 2021, https://www.publishersweekly.com/pw/by-topic/industry-news/religion/article/86832-historian-calls-for-an-evangelical-reckoning-on-race.html.

16. Katherine Kortsmit et al., "Abortion Surveillance—United States, 2019," *Surveillance Summaries* 70, no. 9 (November 26, 2021): 1–29, http://dx.doi.org/10.15585/mmwr.ss7009a1.

17. Diana Greene Foster et al., "Socioeconomic Outcomes of Women Who Receive and Women Who Are Denied Wanted Abortions in the United States," *American Journal of Public Health* 108, no. 3 (March 1, 2018): 407–13, https://ajph.aphapublications.org/doi/full/10.2105/AJPH.2017.304247.

18. Rossi, "Historian Calls for an Evangelical Reckoning on Race."

19. Steven M. Gillon, "Reagan Tied Republicans to White Christians and Now the Party Is Trapped," *The Washington Post*, March 22, 2021, https://www.washingtonpost.com/outlook/2021/03/22/reagan-tied-republicans-white-christians-now-party-is-trapped/.

20. Isaac Kaplan, "Don't Equate Today's Culture Wars to Those of the 1990s," Artsy, December 26, 2017, https://www.artsy.net/article/artsy-editorial-equate-todays-culture-wars-1990s.

21. Estelle Caswell and Mona Lalwani, "The Devilish History of the Explicit Lyrics Sticker," April 26, 2019, https://www.vox.com/videos/2019/4/26/18304456/satan-history-explicit-lyrics-sticker-earworm.

22. "5 Famous Backwards Messages on Records," *College Times*, April 20, 2017, https://ecollegetimes.com/5-famous-backwards-messages-on-records.

23. Karen Swallow Prior, "I Prayed and Protested to End Roe. What Comes Next?" *New York Times*, June 24, 2022, https://www.nytimes.com/2022/06/24/opinion/abortion-dobbs-roe-pro-life.html?fbclid=IwAR2rMDjHk51XSa9hube6cMeXNrjPQMLO3devtIf6R7NcRPGLUv0AFbfPWEc.

24. Alex Samuels, "How Democrats Became Stuck on Immigration," March 30, 2021, FiveThirtyEight, https://fivethirtyeight.com/features/how-democrats-became-stuck-on-immigration/.

25. Ryan Burge, "For White Evangelical Republicans, Approval of Trump Is about Immigration More than Abortion," *Religion in Public* (blog), August 27, 2020, https://religioninpublic.blog/2020/08/27/for-white-evangelical-republicans-approval-of-trump-is-about-immigration-more-than-abortion/.

Chapter 7 Christian Soldiers

1. "Statement from Jericho March: January 14, 2021," Jerichomarch.org, accessed July 1, 2021, https://jerichomarch.org/.

2. Jackson Elliott, "Some Christians Express Concerns over 'Bizarre' Pro-Trump Jericho March," *Christian Post*, December 15, 2020, https://www.christianpost.com /news/some-christians-concerned-over-bizarre-pro-trump-jericho-march.html.

3. Aaron Rupar (@atrupar), "You Can Be Called Up as the Militia to Support & Defend the Constitution," Twitter post, December 12, 2020, https://twitter.com /atrupar/status/1337848438239662085.

4. Daniel A. Cox, "Rise of Conspiracies Reveals an Evangelical Divide in the GOP," The Survey Center on American Life, February 12, 2021, https://www .americansurveycenter.org/rise-of-conspiracies-reveal-an-evangelical-divide-in -the-gop/.

5. "Statement from Jericho March: January 8, 2021," Jerichomarch.org, accessed January 14, 2021, https://jerichomarch.org/.

6. Matthew Avery Sutton, "Donald Trump, the Herald of Evangelicals' End Times," *Seattle Times*, September 30, 2016, https://www.seattletimes.com/opinion /donald-trump-the-herald-of-evangelicals-end-times/.

7. "A Reporter's Footage from inside the Capitol Siege," *New Yorker*, January 17, 2021, https://www.newyorker.com/news/video-dept/a-reporters-footage-from -inside-the-capitol-siege.

8. Jack Jenkins, "The Insurrectionists' Senate Floor Prayer Highlights a Curious Trumpian Ecumenism," Religion News Service, February 25, 2021, https://religion news.com/2021/02/25/the-insurrectionists-senate-floor-prayer-highlights-a-curio us-trumpian-ecumenism/.

9. Jacques Billeaud, "Man Who Wore Horns, Hat Apologizes for Storming Capi- tol," Associated Press, February 9, 2021, https://apnews.com/article/jacob-chansley -apologizes-capitol-riot-66760ebdffe55ea2d9b99965288d80ff.

10. Lexico Dictionaries, s.v. "Patriot," accessed March 7, 2022, https://www.lexico .com/en/definition/patriot.

11. Paul D. Miller, "What Is Christian Nationalism?" *Christianity Today*, Febru- ary 3, 2021, https://www.christianitytoday.com/ct/2021/february-web-only/what-is -christian-nationalism.html.

12. "Christians against Christian Nationalism Statement," Christians Against Christian Nationalism, accessed March 7, 2022, https://www.christiansagainstchr istiannationalism.org/statement.

13. Eugene Scott, "Comparing Trump to Jesus, and Why Some Evangelicals Believe Trump Is God's Chosen One," *The Washington Post*, December 18, 2019, https://www.washingtonpost.com/politics/2019/11/25/why-evangelicals-like-rick -perry-believe-that-trump-is-gods-chosen-one/.

14. Stephen M. Walt, "The Myth of American Exceptionalism," *Foreign Policy*, October 11, 2011, https://foreignpolicy.com/2011/10/11/the-myth-of-american -exceptionalism/.

15. Joseph P. Laycock, "Why So Many Americans Think They're #Blessed," *The Conversation*, April 1, 2016, https://theconversation.com/why-so-many-americans -think-theyre-blessed-54939.

16. Nick Street, "The Kingdom of God and American Exceptionalism," Center for Religion and Civic Culture, April 3, 2017, https://crcc.usc.edu/the-kingdom-of -god-and-american-exceptionalism/.

17. William Doino Jr., "Is America Blessed by God?" *First Things*, August 27, 2012, https://www.firstthings.com/web-exclusives/2012/08/is-america-blessed-by -god.

18. Paul Nathanson, "Review: Myths America Lives By," *Implicit Religion* 7, no. 1 (January 1, 2004).

19. Lucy R. Littler, "The Implications of 'Chosenness': Unsettling the Exodus Narrative as a Model for Black Liberation in Randall Kenan's *A Visitation of Spirits*," *The Southern Literary Journal* 44, no. 1 (2011): 37–55. https://doi.org/10.1353/slj .2011.0018.

20. Peter Moore, "How Would You Fare during the Apocalypse?," YouGov, March 3, 2015, https://today.yougov.com/topics/lifestyle/articles-reports/2015/03/03/how -would-you-fare-apocalypse.

21. Thomas Lecaque, "Trump Has Changed the Way Evangelical Christians Think about the Apocalypse," *The Washington Post*, November 18, 2020, https://www .washingtonpost.com/outlook/2020/11/18/covid-apocalypse-evangelical-christians -election/.

22. Paul S. Boyer, *When Time Shall Be No More: Prophecy Belief in Modern American Culture* (Cambridge, MA: Belknap Press, 2000), 142.

23. James Green, "Reagan, Armageddon & the 1984 Presidential Debate: On the Overlap of Political and Apocalyptic Discourses in America," undergraduate dissertation, University of Bristol, 2009, http://www.bristol.ac.uk/history/media /docs/ug-dissertations/2009green.pdf.

24. Michael Wear, "Why Did Obama Win More White Evangelical Votes than Clinton? He Asked for Them," *The Washington Post*, November 22, 2016, https:// www.washingtonpost.com/posteverything/wp/2016/11/22/why-did-obama-win -more-white-evangelical-votes-than-clinton-he-asked-for-them/.

25. National Association of Evangelicals, "Evangelicals Concur with Obama on Multiple Issues," National Association of Evangelicals, September 28, 2021, https:// www.nae.org/evangelicals-concur-with-obama-on-multiple-issues/.

26. Gregory A. Smith, "More White Americans Adopted than Shed Evangelical Label during Trump Presidency, Especially His Supporters," Pew Research Center, September 15, 2021, https://www.pewresearch.org/fact-tank/2021/09/15/more -white-americans-adopted-than-shed-evangelical-label-during-trump-presidency -especially-his-supporters/.

27. David Brooks, "When Dictators Find God," *New York Times*, September 9, 2021, https://www.nytimes.com/2021/09/09/opinion/autocracy-religion-liber alism.html.

28. Adrienne LaFrance, "The Prophecies of Q," *Atlantic*, June 2020, https://www .theatlantic.com/magazine/archive/2020/06/qanon-nothing-can-stop-what-is-com ing/610567/.

29. Jules Evans, "Nazi Hippies: When the New Age and Far Right Overlap," *GEN*, November 29, 2020, https://gen.medium.com/nazi-hippies-when-the-new-age-and -far-right-overlap-d1a6ddcd7be4.

30. Evans, "Nazi Hippies."

31. Charles King, "I, Too, Was Once a Soldier of the Apocalypse: Why White Evangelicals Must Choose between Reform and American Extremism," *Time*, March 1, 2021, https://time.com/5942445/reform-evangelical-christianity/.

32. Cox, "Rise of Conspiracies Reveals an Evangelical Divide."

33. Tobias Cremer, "Civil Religion vs. White Nationalism: Which Role for Christianity in American Politics?," Berkley Center for Religion, Peace and World Affairs, accessed March 7, 2022, https://berkleycenter.georgetown.edu/responses/civil-religion-vs-white-nationalism-which-role-for-christianity-in-american-politics.

34. Jemar Tisby, "Virtual Author Talk and Q & A with Jemar Tisby," Bethany All-Church Read, lecture, Bethany Presbyterian Church, Seattle, WA, November 15, 2020.

Chapter 8 Work of the People

1. "What Does 'Liturgical' Mean?" Christ Church Lufkin, accessed March 7, 2022, http://christchurchlufkin.com/what-does-liturgical-mean/.

2. Terry Gross and Reynolds Price, "Books: Price's 'Letter to a Godchild,'" *Fresh Air*, June 19, 2006, https://www.npr.org/templates/story/story.php?storyId=5495509.

3. Gina A. Zurlo, Todd M. Johnson, and Peter F. Crossing, "World Christianity and Mission 2020: Ongoing Shift to the Global South," *International Bulletin of Mission Research*, October 16, 2019, https://journals.sagepub.com/doi/full/10.1177/2396939319880074.

4. John Mark Comer and Mark Sayers, *This Cultural Moment* (podcast), accessed July 20, 2022, https://thisculturalmoment.com/.

5. Richard J. Foster, *Celebration of Discipline: The Path to Spiritual Growth* (repr. San Francisco: HarperOne, 2018), 5.

6. Tal Ben-Shahar, *Happier: Learn the Secrets to Daily Joy and Lasting Fulfillment* (Boston: McGraw-Hill, 2007).

Chapter 9 *American* American

1. "General Anthony Wayne Statue Rededicated," City of Fort Wayne Parks and Recreation, accessed March 7, 2022, http://www.fortwayneparks.org/all-2014-releases/633-general-anthony-wayne-statue-rededicated.html.

2. Nell Irvin Painter, *The History of White People* (New York: W.W. Norton, 2011), 366.

3. "Baby Boomers," *History*, May 17, 2010, https://www.history.com/topics/1960s/baby-boomers-1#section_2.

4. Boundless US History, "The Post-War Boom," Lumen Learning, accessed March 7, 2022, https://courses.lumenlearning.com/boundless-ushistory/chapter/culture-of-abundance/.

5. Painter, *History of White People*, 369.

6. Painter, *History of White People*, 366.

7. Tracy Jan, "Redlining Was Banned 50 Years Ago. It's Still Hurting Minorities Today," *The Washington Post*, November 24, 2021, https://www.washingtonpost.com/news/wonk/wp/2018/03/28/redlining-was-banned-50-years-ago-its-still-hurting-minorities-today/.

8. Bruce Mitchell and Juan Franco, "HOLC 'Redlining' Maps: The Persistent Structure of Segregation and Economic Inequality," National Community Reinvestment Coalition, March 20, 2018, https://ncrc.org/holc/.

9. Painter, *History of White People*, 366.

10. Terry Gross, "A 'Forgotten History' of How the U.S. Government Segregated America," *Fresh Air*, May 3, 2017, https://www.npr.org/2017/05/03/526655831/a-forgotten-history-of-how-the-u-s-government-segregated-america.

11. "Redlining in Seattle," Seattle Municipal Archives, accessed May 9, 2022, https://www.seattle.gov/cityarchives/exhibits-and-education/online-exhibits/redlining-in-seattle.

12. Michelle Singletary, "Black Americans Donate a Higher Share of Their Wealth than Whites," *The Washington Post*, December 11, 2020, https://www.washingtonpost.com/business/2020/12/11/blacks-prioritize-philanthropy/.

13. Daniel Silliman, "The Majority of American Megachurches Are Now Multiracial," *Christianity Today*, December 21, 2020, https://www.christianitytoday.com/ct/2021/january-february/multiracial-church-megachurches-race-relations.html.

14. Eileen Luhr, *Witnessing Suburbia: Conservatives and Christian Youth Culture* (Berkeley: University of California Press, 2009), xviii.

15. Luhr, *Witnessing Suburbia*, 18.

16. Luhr, *Witnessing Suburbia*, 13.

17. George Vescey, "Chicago Suburb Is 'Vatican of Evangelicals,'" *New York Times*, July 21, 1978, https://www.nytimes.com/1978/07/21/archives/chicago-suburb-is-vatican-of-evangelicals-a-corporate-christian.html.

18. Vescey, "Chicago Suburb."

19. Tom Wolfe, "Tom Wolfe on the 'Me' Decade in America," *New York Magazine*, repr. April 8, 2008, https://nymag.com/news/features/45938/.

20. Wolfe, "Tom Wolfe on the 'Me' Decade."

21. John Bassett McCleary, *The Hippie Dictionary: A Cultural Encyclopedia (and Phraseicon) of the 1960s and 1970s* (Berkeley, CA: Ten Speed Press, n.d.), 337.

22. Eugene H. Peterson, *A Long Obedience in the Same Direction: Discipleship in an Instant Society* (Downers Grove, IL: IVP, 1980).

23. Ada Calhoun, *Why We Can't Sleep: Women's New Midlife Crisis* (New York: Grove Press, 2020), 37.

24. Aaron Glantz and Emmanuel Martinez, "Modern-Day Redlining: How Banks Block People of Color from Homeownership," *Chicago Tribune*, February 17, 2018, https://www.chicagotribune.com/business/ct-biz-modern-day-redlining-20180215-story.html.

25. William H. Frey, "2020 Census: Big Cities Grew and Became More Diverse, Especially among Their Youth," Brookings, October 28, 2021, https://www.brookings.edu/research/2020-census-big-cities-grew-and-became-more-diverse-especially-among-their-youth/.

Chapter 10 Gold Teeth

1. James C. Dobson, *Life on the Edge: A Young Adult's Guide to a Meaningful Future* (Dallas: Word, 1995).

2. Thomas Schreiner, "Why I Am a Cessationist," The Gospel Coalition, January 22, 2014, https://www.thegospelcoalition.org/article/cessationist/.

3. Will Graham, "MacArthur Accused of Heresy at His Home Church," *Evangelical Focus*, August 19, 2015, https://evangelicalfocus.com/print/903/MacArthur-accused-of-heresy-at-his-home-church.

4. Eskridge, *God's Forever Family*, 40.

5. "About Us," Catch the Fire Church page, accessed March 7, 2022, https://ctftoronto.com/about.

6. Lorna Dueck, "The Enduring Revival," *Christianity Today*, March 7, 2014, https://www.christianitytoday.com/ct/2014/march-web-only/enduring-revival.html.

7. Joe Maxwell, "Is Laughing for the Lord Holy?," *Christianity Today*, October 24, 1994, https://www.christianitytoday.com/ct/1994/october24/4tc078.html.

8. "Larry Norman 11 14 96 TACF Pm," YouTube video, 1:14:22, uploaded by Sober Servant of Praise, May 19, 2021, https://www.youtube.com/watch?v=iuPr6LGDe3I.

9. Sharon Waxman, "Filled with Ho-Ho-Holy Spirit," *The Washington Post*, January 2, 1996, https://www.washingtonpost.com/archive/lifestyle/1996/01/02/filled-with-ho-ho-holy-spirit/aeb5dced-7018-4e70-90b3-6d407885552f/.

10. Waxman, "Filled with Ho-Ho-Holy Spirit."

11. Stoyan Zaimov, "Hank Hanegraaff Must Step Down after Converting to Eastern Orthodoxy: CRI Founder's Family," *Christian Post*, July 14, 2017, https://www.christianpost.com/news/hank-hanegraaff-must-step-down-after-converting-to-eastern-orthodoxy-cri-founders-family.html.

12. Sisters of Notre Dame de Namur, *Visions* (Spring 2013): 1, https://snddenwest.org/wp-content/uploads/sites/5/2013/09/Visions-Spring2013.pdf.

Chapter 11 A Sea of Micro-Authoritarians

1. Christopher Bollen, "Michael Stipe," *Interview*, May 4, 2011, https://www.interviewmagazine.com/music/michael-stipe.

2. Leigh Stein, "The Empty Religions of Instagram," *New York Times*, March 5, 2021, https://www.nytimes.com/2021/03/05/opinion/influencers-glennon-doyle-instagram.html.

3. Glennon Doyle, *Untamed* (New York: Dial Press, 2020).

4. "Why America's 'Nones' Don't Identify with a Religion," Pew Research Center, August 8, 2018, https://www.pewresearch.org/fact-tank/2018/08/08/why-americas-nones-dont-identify-with-a-religion/.

5. Stein, "Empty Religions of Instagram."

6. Leo J. Koffeman, "'Ecclesia Reformata Semper Reformanda' Church Renewal from a Reformed Perspective: Original Research," *HTS: Theological Studies* 73, no. 3, (January 1, 2015), https://journals.co.za/doi/10.4102/hts.v71i3.2875.

7. As quoted in "Simone's Spirit," Rivertext, accessed March 9, 2022, http://rivertext.com/weil3c..html.

Chapter 12 Burnout and the Aspirational Class

1. Anne Helen Petersen, "How Millennials Became the Burnout Generation," *Buzzfeed*, January 5, 2019, https://www.buzzfeednews.com/article/annehelenpetersen/millennials-burnout-generation-debt-work.

2. Derek Thompson, "Workism Is Making Americans Miserable," *Atlantic*, August 13, 2019, https://www.theatlantic.com/ideas/archive/2019/02/religion-workism-making-americans-miserable/583441/.

3. Bill Radke, "March 21st: Burned Out? Here's Some Advice," KUOW, March 21, 2019, https://www.kuow.org/stories/burned-out-here-s-some-advice.

4. Radke, "March 21st."

5. D. Stephen Long, Nancy Ruth Fox, and Tripp York, *Calculated Futures: Theology, Ethics, and Economics* (Waco: Baylor University Press, 2007), 187.

6. William T. Cavanaugh, *Being Consumed: Economics and Christian Desire* (Grand Rapids: Eerdmans, 2009), 34.

7. Cavanaugh, *Being Consumed*, 34.

8. Shankar Vedantam, "Never Go to Vegas," *Hidden Brain*, March 18, 2019, https://www.npr.org/transcripts/704416322.

9. Petersen, "How Millennials Became the Burnout Generation."

10. Kaitlyn Tiffany, "Kanye West Hosted a Coachella Easter Service Featuring $225 Sweatshirts," *Vox*, April 22, 2019, https://www.vox.com/the-goods/2019/4/22/18511175/kanye-west-easter-service-coachella-church-clothes-merch.

11. "Millennials Want Experiences over Products," Companjon, accessed March 8, 2022, https://www.companjon.com/news/millennials-want-experiences/.

12. Cindy Wooden, "'Capitalism Gives a Moral Cloak to Inequality,' Pope Francis Says at Italian Steel Plant," *America*, May 30, 2017, https://www.americamagazine.org/faith/2017/05/30/capitalism-gives-moral-cloak-inequality-pope-francis-says-italian-steel-plant.

13. "Peace Prayer of Saint Francis," Loyola Press, accessed March 7, 2022, https://www.loyolapress.com/catholic-resources/prayer/traditional-catholic-prayers/saints-prayers/peace-prayer-of-saint-francis/. Public domain.

Chapter 13 Burned but Not Consumed

1. Flannery O'Connor, *Habit of Being* (New York: Farrar, Straus & Giroux, 1999), 308.

2. Justo L. Gonzalez, *The Story of Christianity: The Early Church to the Reformation* (New York: HarperOne, 2010), 187.

3. Craig L. Nessan, "Learning from the Barmen Declaration of 1934: Theological-Ethical-Political Commentary," *Journal of Lutheran Ethics*, December 1, 2019, https://elca.org/JLE/Articles/1292?gclid=CjwKCAiAv_KMBhAzEiwAs-rX1CIQSivTGv77OcyGPHB66tN34FJbiDe4Ned00ON0aT3jcMcMLaEODBoCIw0QAvD_BwE.

4. Lindsey and Carlson, *Late Great Planet Earth*, 188.

5. Elizabeth Dias, "'Christianity Will Have Power': How a Promise by Trump Bonded Him to White Evangelicals," *New York Times*, August 9, 2020, https://www.nytimes.com/2020/08/09/us/evangelicals-trump-christianity.html.

6. Dallas Willard, "Spiritual Formation: What it is, and How it is Done," *Dallas Willard*, accessed June 10, 2022, https://dwillard.org/articles/spiritual-formation-what-it-is-and-how-it-is-done.

7. "Burning Bush," Presbyterian Church in Ireland, accessed June 13, 2022, https://www.oxfordreference.com/view/10.1093/acref/9780199916191.001.0001/acref-9780199916191-e-0207.

Sara Billups is a Seattle-based writer and cultural commentator whose work has appeared in the *New York Times*, *Christianity Today*, *Ekstasis*, and others. Sara serves on the vestry at her local church and is completing a Doctor of Ministry in the sacred art of writing at the Eugene Peterson Center for Christian Imagination at Western Theological Seminary.